LIMITLESS POSSIBILITIES

AYO AJAYI

LIMITLESS POSSIBILITIES

Published in the United States by Eclecticgrace LLC
Houston Texas

Inquiries:
www.transformwithayo.com

Email: Limitlesspossibilities24@gmail.com

All Scripture quotations are taken from King James Version (KJV), New King James Version (NKJV), The Message (MSG) and the New Living Translation (NLT)

Contents

Acknowledgment

All thanks, praise, and acknowledgment go to the Author, and the Giver of life who has blessed and surrounded me with great, loving, and amazing people whose input made this mission a reality. Over the years they have believed in, encouraged, challenged, and prodded me to capture my sermons, quotes, and thoughts into a book, and what you are now holding is the result; the first of many more to come.

I appreciate my lovely wife, Olayide Oluwakemi Ajayi for her selfless love and support in and out of season as I strive to express my calling and gifts in varying seasons. I am grateful to my gorgeous children, Omotola, Oluwabukola, and Ayoolaoluwa for the inspiration I always draw from them. They are a bundle of joy to me and I love them dearly for their understanding during those times when I wasn't available for them.

Moreover, I want to thank my late parents, Pa Clement Falade and Ma Grace Abeke Ajayi; my number one fans. They believed in me and always encouraged me even when there was nothing believable about me. I am eternally grateful for their unwavering confidence in me at all times.

I also appreciate my parents-in-law, Prof. Tunde and Mrs. Helen Tegbe for their genuine constant love, encouragement, and support always.

I am grateful for the entire household of faith RCCG SALVATION CENTER KATY TEXAS, for their exceptional support through the period I was writing this book. I thank God for my dynamic and able assistants Pastors Shola, and Fisayo

Adegoke for standing by me at all times. I appreciate the council of ministers, the entire workforce, and the members of the Salvation Center Katy family for their inspiration, support, and love. I want to also acknowledge all my friends and family that have believed in me and cheered me on over the years.

I do appreciate and acknowledge the covering, leadership, and mentorship of my father in the Lord the General Overseer of RCCG worldwide, Pastor E.A Adeboye, and the Continental Overseer (CO) for RCCG The Americas (North, Central & South), Pastor James Fadel; all my mentors both virtual and physical and all my colleagues for their unfeigned support in and out of season, thank you very much.

I acknowledge the team that worked day and night to review and edit this work to make it what it is today.

Finally, I want to appreciate my friend and sister, Pastor Joy Lifechangers, for being the engine behind the success of this book project. She motivated, galvanized, and compelled me to complete this project. Her friendship and support have been invaluable and I am truly grateful!

Dedication

This book is dedicated to the Almighty God who has blessed me with life and resources to make this book a dream come true. It is also dedicated to my lovely wife, Olayide Ajayi, my two wonderful daughters Tola and Bukola, and my one and only son Ayoolaoluwa.

Introduction

Imagine I offered you a blank check or a debit card that had no withdrawal limit and told you to use it whenever, wherever, and however you pleased.

As long as you do not waste the gift, and put it to good use, a giver may not care if you are considerate or reckless with the gift.

I know some people may be considerate of their spending because the card isn't theirs. The reality is it is a gift. As long as you do not waste the gift, and put it to good use, the giver does not care how much of the gift you use. The giver is more excited when you use this card because it is flowing from an inexhaustible fountain. You are actually doing the giver a favor and giving them great joy by using it.

If you were offered such a limitless lifetime opportunity, what would the quality of your life look like? What plans or dreams would you execute? Where will you choose to shop? What kind of car will you drive? What kind of house will you live in? What kind of business will you invest in? Would it matter whether the economy was down or not? Would you worry or become anxious if you were running out of anything?

Let's assume that this card or check could buy you a blissful married life and wonderful family, a twelve-figure job, and sound health. What if it could wipe out all your terrible past and eliminate any adverse effects on your future? And what if it could buy you time, provide emotional balance, manifest your dream spouse, get you out of jail, and make your past mistakes inconsequential? Suppose it could also give you a wonderful family with the best-behaved children, a vibrant spiritual life, redeem your life from death, and create the most prosperous future for you. If all you had to do was to tender or swipe this card whenever you had a need, would you settle for anything less?

This is exactly what an invitation to salvation has to offer. It is an invitation to the abundant life that overflows with milk and honey. It is a lifetime of limitless opportunity that is unfathomable, inestimable, and inexhaustible.

Unfortunately, that is not the case with many believers. We live in the ocean, yet die of thirst. We live in the realm of limitless possibilities but live a life below expectations. This is indeed an error of the highest degree.

Ecclesiastes 10:5-7 AMP

5 There is an evil I have seen under the sun, like an error which proceeds from the ruler—
6 folly is set in many exalted places and in great dignity while the rich sit in humble places.
7 I have seen slaves riding on horses and princes walking like slaves on the ground.

God El Shaddai, the double-breasted one is in excruciating pain like a lactating mother whose breast is overflowing with milk but whose child isn't willing to suck, yet the breast keeps producing milk without ceasing. Consider it this way, it's like a parent who has so much wealth but their children choose to suffer and would not take advantage of the parent's wealth because they want to prove that they can succeed on their own.

How many of us can bear witnessing our children endure suffering when we have the means to assist them, yet they refuse to accept our help? This would be torturous and quite painful for me as a parent. The reality is that parents endure immense hardship when they witness their children refusing their offer of help and needlessly suffering as they try to navigate challenges independently. This is exactly what we put God through whenever we ignore the free gift of grace without measure that He has made available for us as His children.

Two distinct occasions can be found within the scriptures where Jesus wept in frustration as he observed the children of Israel failing to fully realize the blessings bestowed upon them by God, largely due to their ignorance. On one occasion, they did not recognize the day of their visitation. They were unwittingly contending against the very Jesus who was intended to be their solution and deliver them from their oppression. They opted for a murderer over a savior, choosing Barabbas instead of Jesus. On another occasion, Jesus wept at the tomb of Lazarus because He couldn't help them comprehend the truth that they were unstoppable, even in the face of death, if only they could believe. This is the ordeal we subject God to when we fail to seize the abundant blessings and plans He has in store for us.

There has to be a point in time when we start taking advantage of the free gifts that God has made available for us to put an end to our suffering and relieve God of the frustration of watching us suffer while living a life that is below average. The prodigal son came to himself and turned his fortune around!
(Luke 15:17)

Romans 8:32 (KJV)
He that spared not his own Son, but delivered him up for us all, how shall he not with him also freely give us all things?

Romans 8:31-33 (MSG)
So, what do you think? With God on our side like this, how can we lose? If God didn't hesitate to put everything on the line for us, embracing our condition and exposing himself to the worst

by sending his own Son, is there anything else he wouldn't gladly and freely do for us?
And who would dare tangle with God by messing with one of God's chosen?
Who would dare even to point a finger?
The One who died for us—
who was raised to life for us!—is in the presence of God at this very moment sticking up for us.

This passage implies that if God could give up His only begotten son to redeem us from darkness when we didn't deserve it, there is nothing that He will not do to ensure we live the best of life. He will leave no stone unturned! Like the popular song Reckless Love by Cory Asbury

- "There is no shadow He won't light up, mountain He won't climb up, coming after me! There is no wall He won't kick down, lie He won't tear down coming after me..."

He does all these and more to make sure we maximize our divine destiny.

This book is dedicated to illuminating the pathway to a realm of boundless limitless possibilities, where all things are achievable and nothing can hinder us from realizing our dreams & aspirations once we set our minds and hearts to achieve them.

Genesis 11:6 (KJV)

6: And the Lord said, Behold, the people is one, and they have all one language; and this they begin to do: and now nothing will be restrained from them, which they have imagined to do.

This scripture above means we have the capacity and potential to accomplish whatever we can imagine. The good news is that our dreams, visions & aspirations readily available to us, seamlessly and free of charge.

Romans 8:32 implies that He will freely GIVE US ALL THINGS WITH JESUS. That means Salvation is not the only thing that the death and the resurrection of Jesus Christ can afford us. It is just the starting point and the gateway to ALL THINGS. Everything we can ever imagine is also included in the package. The Jesus who freely gave us salvation is also the one who will generously provide us with everything we could ever desire in life, without cost.

This book is crafted to liberate us from self-imposed defeat, to guide us in embracing adversities as opportunities, and to empower us to surmount any limitations on our journey toward realizing our desires and dreams in life.

CHAPTER 1

ALL THINGS ARE POSSIBLE

It is possible! All things are possible!! Nothing is impossible!! Impossibility does not exist!!

While it might sound cliché or far-fetched, it's crucial that we acknowledge and wholeheartedly embrace this truth as the ordained reality that God has designed for us. All the extraordinary miracles chronicled in the Bible are not merely tales or works of fiction. These are actual events supported by evidence, documented to serve as examples and encouragement for those of us facing similar circumstances. If we follow the same pathway, we will definitely experience the same order of results.

The Red Sea parted for the children of Israel to walk through on dry land and water came out of the rock to quench their thirst. God fed the children of Israel miraculously for forty years, and their shoes and clothes supernaturally grew as they grew in age without wearing out for forty years. Ninety-year-old Sarah gave birth to a child. The fortune of a nation was turned around in 24 hrs from slaves to having great possessions; the lame walked, the blind saw, the dead were raised, a woman was pregnant without having sex with a man, and countless other mysterious miracles. These are all well-documented events that truly occurred.

Therefore, regardless of how old you are, you can still find and marry the spouse of your dream! Ruth, the daughter-in-law of Naomi, discovered Boaz and emerged from a state of hopelessness to become the great-grandmother of Jesus. Regardless of your age, you can still birth your biological child! I will refer you to Sarah and Abraham. If you inquire of Esther and the three Hebrew boys, you'll realize that regardless of immigration status, success is attainable anywhere in the world.

The earth is the Lord's and its fullness thereof. He has said that He will give you wherever the sole of your feet shall tread upon. You can come out of prison and still become the prime minister of your nation, ask Joseph and Nelson Mandela. You can be homeless today and still own an apartment complex tomorrow, ask Obed Edom. Your business could face bankruptcy today but transform into a global brand tomorrow. Your history does not have to limit the success of your future. It is not over until it is over. All things are possible with God!

WHEN GOD SAYS YES

I remember the story of a spirit-filled joyful couple, who before tying the knot, received a divine assurance from God that they would be blessed with both male and female children. After they got married and started having children they had three girls. They prayed and decided that they were going to try just one more time after which they would stop completely. They welcomed their fourth child, only to find themselves blessed with another daughter. They then assumed and concluded that they probably didn't hear God right and got it wrong. As intended, they concluded their journey of childbearing and opted for a procedure known as tubal ligation to permanently close the wife's fallopian tubes. The positive aspect is that their desire for a male child was not driven by desperation or bias that a male child is superior to a female child. It was from the standpoint of trying to execute the will of God based on what they thought they heard from Him. They relinquished their dream of having a male child and proceeded with their lives contentedly. Despite their initial preference not to have more than three children they wholeheartedly committed to caring for their four beautiful daughters to the best of their ability. Mysteriously, a year later, the wife became pregnant despite having undergone tubal ligation. Medical experts advised the couple to terminate the pregnancy due to significant risks to both the baby and the mother's health. They chose to proceed with the pregnancy, as terminating it went against their religious beliefs. They also opted not to determine the sex of the baby because they wanted to avoid potential disappointment.

Miraculously, the pregnancy survived its gestation period. They arrived at the hospital on the anticipated delivery date, unsure of what to expect – whether the baby would be deformed as speculated by medical experts or what the sex of the baby would be. Their prayers this time encompassed not only the sex of the baby but also the health and well-being of both the baby and the mother.

To the glory of God, the baby was delivered safely and both the baby and the mother were perfectly well. Guess what, it was a cute baby boy! Both parents cried profusely and the medical team around them could not understand why. They wondered why something that should bring joy was instead bringing tears to their eyes. They had no inkling that their tears were tears of joy, marveling at what only God could have accomplished. What had been deemed impossible became possible under extraordinary circumstances. Glory to God!

NATURAL MINDSET

We are in a world where crazy things happen daily because of the limits life has imposed on us. In recent years, the coronavirus pandemic has claimed numerous lives and left many individuals and businesses grappling with uncertainty. It triggered an unprecedented global financial crisis, resulting in inflation and recession that have severely impacted the world economy.

Every measure implemented to address the situation has only served to exacerbate the issue and worsen the circumstances. Regrettably, no definitive solution seems to be at hand, with blame being placed on the government and various other entities.

People are experiencing heightened emotions, with shootings on the rise, divorce rates soaring, crime rates spiraling out of control, and alarming increases in suicide rates across the board.

The root cause of these unfortunate events lies in our response — a propensity to accept restrictions, limitations, and perceived impossibilities imposed by human nature.

Natural behavior dictates that when we encounter situations beyond our control and struggle to find a solution, we often react negatively, responding in ways that are inconsistent with actions that could potentially improve the situation. In certain cases, when we feel devoid of options or when it seems we've lost control, our natural inclination is to resort to temper tantrums or behave erratically.

On the other hand, adopting the right perspective and attitude — taking control of what we can control and surrendering what we can't to God — would likely lead to positive outcomes and initiate a process to manage the things beyond our control. For instance, rather than allowing yourself to become overwhelmed with worry and depression while trying to reverse an irreversible medical condition outlined in an unfavorable doctor's report — something beyond your control — it's more beneficial to concentrate on what you can control. This might involve praying and fasting, confessing and applying healing scriptures relevant to the situation, adhering to prescribed medication, expressing gratitude for other blessings bestowed by God, and entrusting the miraculous to God's providence.

This is the principle that most people call "mind your business". So if we focus on our business and attend to what we can control, entrusting the rest to God, many of our worries will be resolved supernaturally. The Bible says, tomorrow will take care of itself if we stop worrying.

NOT BACKING DOWN

All things are possible! No problem is impossible. Some challenges are labeled as impossible not because they're inherently unsolvable, but because they're reserved as opportunities for the select few who refuse to accept defeat. Those aspiring for greatness and specialization at the pinnacle of their chosen field cannot afford to retreat when faced with obstacles. They must perceive all obstacles as opportunities. Impossibilities are henceforth classified as gateways to greatness.

From experience, I've noticed that many of us tend to give up easily when confronted with complex questions that seem to have no answers readily available. Such a habit is a barrier to achieving greatness

I remember when I was in high school, only students who wanted to become engineers studied further mathematics as their major. I must acknowledge that it was an exceedingly challenging course, not suited for the lazy or those prone to giving up easily. We had to deal with calculus. Whenever we are given problems that are very difficult, Some of us would not even attempt to solve the problems at all but would rather wait for others we perceive as smarter to solve it first and copy it verbatim. Some of us abandoned attempts to solve the problems after numerous failed tries, while others became utterly frustrated and ultimately dropped out of the class, relinquishing their dream of becoming engineers. But a handful of us brainstormed and collaborated to find a solution to the problem, and they eventually succeeded in resolving it! The problem being eventually solved by the persistent, hard-working few students who refused to back down proved wrong those of us who believed the problem had no solution. Some people believed it couldn't be solved by individuals within our peer group, but guess what? The equation was successfully solved by our colleagues who chose to take on the challenge.

In retrospect, I realized that the teacher who assigned the questions already had the answers to the equations before giving them to us. This indicates that the problem was not an insurmountable task. He presented us with challenging questions to stimulate and enhance our intellectual capacity, assessing our level of understanding and comprehension. This enabled him to strategically and progressively guide us toward greatness. This experience instilled within us a deeper sense of focus and determination, propelling us toward our destined path of greatness. In hindsight, we recognize that the teacher's actions were instrumental in shaping our journey and equipping us for the challenges that lay ahead.

Now, I've come to realize that your willingness to take on and overcome challenges determines your altitude in life.This distinction separates high achievers from the mediocre, the average from the low class. As long as we inhabit this earth, we'll encounter various limitations on our path to greatness or in achieving extraordinary results. How we respond to these limitations determines whether we'll seize the opportunity they present or let them hinder our progress.

HOW SHALL THIS BE?

This is the kind of question that arises whenever we face humanly impossible Problem.

Let us consider a case study in

Luke 1:30-34 (KJV)

And the angel said unto her, Fear not, Mary: for thou hast found favor with God.

And, behold, thou shalt conceive in thy womb and bring forth a son, and shalt call his name Jesus.

He shall be great, and shall be called the Son of the Highest: and the Lord God shall give unto him the throne of his father David:

And he shall reign over the house of Jacob forever; and of his kingdom, there shall be no end.

Then said Mary unto the angel, How shall this be, seeing I know not a man?

This is the story of a young woman that was presented with the responsibility of producing greatness and helping the accomplishment of one of humanity's greatest goals and dreams under absolutely impossible circumstances.

In this passage, the Angel Gabriel appeared to Mary and conveyed the extraordinary news that she would conceive a child without engaging in any form of sexual intercourse or artificial insemination. This announcement directly contradicted the established principles of conception and reproduction as understood by medical science. Faced with this scientific limitation, Mary expressed her disbelief to the angel, stating that what he had conveyed seemed utterly impossible, as it contradicted the well-known biological process wherein a man and a woman is required to engage in sexual intercourse in order to conceive and bear children.

With the benefit of hindsight, what Mary said was impossible was actually made possible by God. Mary did give birth to Jesus without having intercourse with any man. This proves that nothing is impossible! Science or technologies are wrong! They are not the final authority on any matter. Wherever there is a will there's a way! God can make a way where there seems no way.

All the stories in the Bible are not just mere stories or historical fiction that were made up for us to enjoy, or for our information only. They were events that happened in real life and were captured through the inspiration of the Holy Ghost. These stories are packaged as spiritual principles or blueprints to be followed in order to get the same outcomes. This means if we follow the same principle as Mary we will get the same result that Mary got whenever we face any impossible situation.

Mary's problem was a very complex one because it was three-dimensional **(3D-PROBLEM).**

The first obstacle confronting her was the stark opposition of scientific principles, which seemed to outright reject the possibility of her breakthrough.

The second dilemma loomed large - even if she managed to

circumvent scientific norms, she would still face the formidable barrier of societal laws that strictly prohibited bearing a child out of wedlock. Such a transgression was met with severe consequences, tantamount to a death sentence for both her and the child. Thus, defying scientific limitations alone was not enough to ensure her safety.

The third challenge, perhaps the most emotionally daunting, was the prospect of enduring the shame and abandonment by her fiancé, friends, and family. The bleak reality of being ostracized from her community, deemed unworthy of marriage, and left to raise the child alone weighed heavily on her shoulders. The repercussions of this social isolation could have far-reaching implications for her future.
These three-dimensional obstacles painted a grim picture of the daunting journey ahead, casting doubt on the feasibility of the angel's message. From a purely human perspective, the circumstances seemed utterly insurmountable. It appeared inconceivable that Jesus' birth could occur without the intervention of supernatural forces.

There are so many people in the world today in the same situation as Mary; asking the same question "HOW SHALL THIS BE"? due to the intricate nature of the constraints restricting the potential for achieving their desired outcome. I have good news for you - "Welcome to the "Realm of Limitless Possibilities?" where all things are possible! Where many "How shall this be?" concerns are addressed and resolved without fail. Some people have questions like how will I find a life partner and be able to get married seeing I don't have the Hollywood looks? Age is not on my side and been through years of delayed promises with nothing coming forth.

How can I ever regain control of my life or improve upon it, especially considering my past prison record or history that seems to be hindering my present situation?

How can I recover my health seeing that every medical report is bleak with impossible odds? How can I put an end to this cycle of struggle, living hand-to-mouth, especially when I lack any viable means of livelihood? How shall I pay off my debt without a thriving business?

How can I bounce back from failure and successfully graduate from college, when it's evident from the academic policy that there's seemingly no possible scenario for me to graduate?

How can I revive my situation when it's not just dead, decayed, or rotten, but the bones are completely dried? (Ezekiel 37).

How can I possibly restore my marriage when we've gone from separation to divorce? Our hope of reconciliation seems as distant as the east is from the west, especially since my spouse has already begun the process of marrying someone else.

How can I have my peace back and sleep well at night without medication, seeing I am addicted to a life of horror and oppression?

How can I bear my children seeing that I have no womb or no spam count; I am sterile or infertile?

How can I be spiritually alive again and be fully revived, seeing that I have done some abominable things? I kept on falling and failing God.

How can I recover from bankruptcy, repossession, and foreclosure seeing I no longer have a means of livelihood?

I have good news for you. Welcome to the **"Kingdom of Limitless Possibilities"** where the word impossibility has been deleted from our vocabulary! The realm where you can do all things through Christ; you can become anything you dare to believe God for.

A kingdom where you can get as far as your eyes can see. A kingdom that offers you a blank check for everything you need! Unlimited opportunities are an opportunity to operate with a blank check where you are the one that decides what is written on the check.

The way the kingdom works is strange and unique. It is a situation where you don't need to be likely to succeed in order to succeed. This means you will not only win possible battles but also impossible battles. You will always be faced with questionable situations or circumstances that challenge the possibilities of your breakthrough and could make you ask questions like "How shall this be" because, under all circumstances, every chance for a possibility has been disqualified beyond redemption.

Therefore, the divine expo or Intel you are receiving as you read this book is that you should not freak out when impossibilities knock at your door, they are blessings in disguise. They are hidden treasures or miracles buried within the obstacles or challenges waiting for discovery.

Isaiah 45:3 (KJV)

And I will give thee the treasures of darkness, and hidden riches of secret places, that thou mayest know that I, the LORD, which call thee by thy name, am the God of Israel.

In the kingdom, you'll encounter numerous opportunities disguised as challenges or setbacks. Some doors may seem shut with adversaries and obstacles blocking your path. You might face seemingly impossible choices, yet these are blessings in disguise. Your marriage won't show visible signs of progress before experiencing a complete turnaround and restoration. Everything will unfold suddenly and inexplicably, but it will be attributable to your unwavering faith journey.

Your career will suddenly take off from below ground zero at a time when it seemed to have nose-dived at an alarming rate, this will happen in a way that is not traceable to your experience or certification.

Your business will explode globally from that state of bankruptcy and helplessness when your back seems against the wall and it looks like everything is over.

You may not recover your health when the condition is getting better but at the terminal stage total restoration will happen. When the bone is completely dried in the grave; suddenly a great army will arise.

Your child's grade will skyrocket and their attitude will become the best at the point of lowest probability for reversibility.

Your immigration status will change with or without favorable changes in government policy. You will pay off your debt mysteriously, come out of prison majestically, and turn your life around despite all the odds stacked against you.

You will not have to put on makeup or get all dressed up, you may even be the most unlikely to be selected when you will meet your Boaz this year. You may not remember to do your quiet time that morning, it may not be your most spiritual day. It may even be an ordinary day when you least expect it and when there is a "no way it is possible" situation at hand. That's when the Holy Ghost goes to work - (an unstoppable wind that blows where it wishes; the rushing mighty wind that parted the red sea; the east wind that blows to make a way where there is no way) and the highest order of power is released.

CHAPTER 2

SUPERNATURAL AWARENESS OF THE UNSEEN REALM

The Two Marketplaces of Life

1 Corinthians 15:19 (TPT)
If the only benefit of our hope in Christ is limited to this life on earth, we deserve to be pitied more than all others!

1 Corinthians 15:19 (KJV)
If in this life only we have hope in Christ, we are of all men most miserable.

If what determines or sustains the state of our hope is only what is humanly possible on earth, we will experience the highest degree of frustration and be graded in the class of the most miserable people on earth.

There are two marketplaces available for believers to shop in. First, the natural marketplace where humanly possible items are displayed. Second, the **supernatural marketplace** where humanly impossible items are displayed.

Think about the exclusivity of name brands, impossible items are the branded class displayed and sold at the supernatural marketplace in the heavenly places. While humanly possible items are the non-branded class displayed in the natural marketplace here on earth.

If we restrict our desires to items that are only naturally possible, we limit ourselves to shopping for items that are only humanly possible in this life. As a result, we will miss out on the extraordinary opportunities reserved on the rack of impossibility in life, consequently settling for mediocrity and falling short of the best that God has in store for us.

1 Corinthians 2:12 (NKJV)
Now we have received, not the spirit of the world, but the spirit which is of God; that we might know the things that are freely ***given to us of God.***

Everything is freely made available for us by God to be enjoyed right here on earth. The scripture delves deeper into the notion that if we only expect what's attainable in the natural realm, we will miss out on many great opportunities that are routed through the pathway of impossibilities exclusively. If this is the only consequence involved, navigating life would be less complex. The main frustration stems from an innate, insatiable hunger planted within us by God - a yearning for more daily, knowing that we have greater potential and deserve a better existence.

This scripture serves as a gauge, measuring the intensity of our misery and frustration. Just as in language we have degrees of beauty—beautiful, more beautiful, and most beautiful—similarly, we have varying levels of misery—miserable, more miserable, and most miserable. The initial level of frustration applies to those unable to afford their basic needs, such as individuals aspiring for higher-paying jobs but lacking the necessary qualifications due to limited education.

The subsequent tier experiences heightened frustration; these individuals possess the means to afford their desires but face disqualification due to societal marginalization or injustice. They may be qualified for better positions but encounter barriers like immigration status, racial discrimination, or past criminal records.

However, believers find themselves among the most frustrated. Deep within us lies the conviction that we're capable of achieving more, empowered by a God who transcends barriers like racial discrimination, immigration status, or past mistakes. We possess the spiritual tools to overcome any obstacle, yet often fall short in our spiritual diligence to seize the best options available to us. Thus, our frustration stems not from external limitations but from our own spiritual inertia, hindering us from accessing the abundant blessings that await us.

1 Corinthians 2:9 (NKJV)
But as it is written:
"Eye has not seen, nor ear heard, Nor have entered into the heart of man the things which God has prepared for those who love Him."

According to the Bible, what God has in store for us is unparalleled and beyond comprehension; it's so extraordinary that no eye has seen, no ear has heard, and no human heart has conceived of its magnificence.

This divine provision is like an exclusive reservation, reserved only for us. Therefore, when faced with challenges and told that a solution doesn't exist, we must remain steadfast. If what awaits us is unseen by human eyes, it's natural for others to doubt its existence and declare our situation as unsolvable. We need not be alarmed when told our circumstances are uniquely difficult or unprecedented. Whenever we encounter the word "impossible," let's replace it with **"exclusively reserved."** This mindset shift reminds us that our destiny holds something extraordinary, beyond the limitations of human understanding. So, let's hold fast to faith, knowing that what awaits us is reserved exclusively for us by divine decree.

Your purpose in this world transcends accomplishing just what is humanly possible; you are also meant to achieve the seemingly impossible. If your endeavors in life are limited solely to what is within human capacity, you render yourself redundant and risk squandering the unique opportunity of doing life bestowed upon you by divine grace. Consider the staggering odds you defied to claim your place in this world—out of millions of competing spermatozoa, you emerged victorious, chosen for a specific purpose. Therefore, it's imperative that you make the most of this precious gift of life, by pushing beyond the boundaries of what seems attainable to accomplish the extraordinary.

Each of us is intricately designed for a specific purpose, and many of the challenges we encounter in life are intricately linked to fulfilling that divine purpose. When we stray from our unique assignment to pursue tasks already undertaken by others, we compromise our unique value proposition and risk being deemed redundant. It's vital not to veer off course and pursue the path of least resistance simply because we encounter obstacles along the way. Instead, we're called to confront and overcome these obstacles head-on and doggedly, demonstrating resilience and determination.

In the realm of employment, redundancy occurs when an employee repetitively performs tasks or responsibilities that have already been addressed. This diminishes their value and often leads to layoffs. Similarly, when purchasing appliances, manufacturers sometimes include redundant components — extras that serve as backups in case of component failure. While these redundant components may provide a sense of security, they ultimately hold little value as there are already sufficient components performing the same function effectively.

Likewise, straying from our unique purpose in pursuit of easier paths or tasks already undertaken by others renders us ineffective and diminishes our value. We must remain steadfast in our commitment to fulfilling our purpose, confronting challenges head-on, and refusing to be deterred by obstacles along the way. Failure to rise to the occasion not only undermines our potential but also diminishes the impact we're meant to have in the world.

Luke 13:7 (NKJV)

Then he said to the keeper of his vineyard, 'Look, for three years I have come seeking fruit on this fig tree and find none. Cut it down; why does it use up the ground?'

According to Luke 13:7, the trees that were competing for and wasting the nutrients from the ground without producing value were required to be cut down and burnt with fire.

OVERCOMING LIMITATIONS

1 Corinthians 16:9 (NKJV)

For a great and effective door has opened to me, and there are many adversaries.

Paul said in the verse above that great doors have been opened but there are many limitations! Many of these limitations serve as a strategic means to deter us from succeeding or to induce frustration leading us to abandon our God-given dreams. Only those who defy these limitations will access greatness in life.

In our journey through life, we encounter various limitations stemming from scientific laws, technological constraints, medical advancements, psychological barriers shaped by our experiences, societal norms and events, governmental regulations, and environmental factors.

These limitations often feel like a prison, dictating the boundaries of our existence and setting limits on our potential. However, for those who are in Christ Jesus, this paradigm shifts dramatically. According to John 8:32, the truth sets us free from the shackles of these limitations.

As a consequence, as children of God, we are liberated from the grip of all forms of restriction. Anything that suggests otherwise is a falsehood. With God on our side, nothing can hinder us; indeed, nothing can prevail against us (Romans 8:31).

Hence, the freedom we have in Christ is absolute and undeniable. As stated in John 8:36, "So if the Son sets you free, you will be free indeed with proof and without any limitations." This freedom transcends mere belief — it is a tangible reality, experienced and lived without constraints or limitations.

Romans 8:1-2 (KJV)

There is, therefore (now!) no condemnation (limitations) to them which are in Christ Jesus, who walk not after the flesh, but after the Spirit.

For the law of the Spirit of life in Christ Jesus hath made me free from the law of sin and death.

This scripture is saying, even right now, the people of God are not limited in any capacity and therefore, nothing should be impossible for them. They do not walk in the natural, they walk in the spirit. Therefore, whatever restrict the natural people cannot limit them.

For us to maximize the opportunities provided by God for us in the world of unlimited possibilities, we need to be fully aware of this exclusive promise and maximize it by engaging spiritual principles instead of bowing to the limitation of natural principles. Spiritual principles are an upgrade on natural principles because they thrive where natural principles fail.

Examining the trajectory of history, it's evident that nothing is truly beyond the realm of possibility. Many feats or advancements once deemed impossible have become possible through the course of time, thanks to the ongoing discoveries, innovations and advancements of science and technology. In hindsight, it seems these accomplishments were never truly impossible; rather, they were labeled as such due to our limited understanding or lack of knowledge at that time.

What we once perceived as insurmountable obstacles were, in reality, challenges awaiting innovative solutions. Our perception of impossibility stemmed from a lack of solution or insight necessary to achieve them because we were unaware of the transformative power of redemption. Through divine enlightenment bestowed upon us through the revelation of God's word, we now recognize that nothing is inherently absolutely impossible. It's merely a matter of time before the solution emerges and what was once deemed impossible becomes a tangible reality.

Hence, Impossibilities can therefore be regarded as issues with the solutions awaiting discovery. Do you realize how many lives have been lost, devastations or destructions that have occurred, and most importantly how many opportunities have been missed or wasted because we had the wrong conclusion that it was impossible? Instead of accepting defeat when we are faced with limitations; with the right perspective, we should devote our energy to removing the limitation and seek the solution that is readily available. This should be the rule of the game and should be applied to every impossibility that has existed and could ever exist. Nothing is absolutely impossible; we just need to search out the solution.

DISCOVERY MINDSET

The term "discovery" implies that the solution was not newly created but rather already existed and is now being found or unveiled. You can only discover what already exists! This suggests that every problem's solution already exists somewhere in the universe, awaiting discovery by a determined individual. The existence of a solution implies that someone has envisioned and conceptualized the problem, devising a remedy before its manifestation. This principle applies not only to specific issues but also to potential challenges faced by individuals.

Based on the track record of God, He is a proactive God and not a reactive God. A great example is the scenario of the sad event that happened to Adam and Eve in the Garden of Eden and the joyful event of Jesus Christ's sacrifice on the cross of Calvary. Based on the scripture, it is written that the Lamb was slain before the foundation of the world. This means that God had already envisaged the fall of man and made provision for our deliverance even before the incident happened. This is the modus operandi of God with science and technology often trailing behind, uncovering what God has already done and labeling it as discovery.

Proverbs 25:2 (KJV)
It is the glory of God to conceal a thing: but the honor of kings is to search out a matter.

Proverbs 25:2 (MSG)
God delights in concealing things; scientists delight in discovering things.

Can you see that scientists are smarter than believers? They do always keep searching until they can find an answer. God has no option but to give them access because His children are just too lazy to search. Believers are generally spoiled and complacent.

He has to give the unbelieving scientist access to the crumbs that fall from the children's table to keep the system running till the believer gets it right. Can you imagine what the actual bread will do if we take advantage of it? The Bible says "Unto us it is given to discover the mystery of the kingdom but not unto them." (Mark 4:11).

Unfortunately, no matter how much they search, there are certain things they will never discover which are exclusively reserved for the eyes of the Spirit to search out. Answers to all impossibilities already exist, we just need to diligently search them out. God has a huge sense of humor. He likes playing hide-and-seek games. He hides a thing and expects us to search it out. Unfortunately when we can't find it, we assume that it doesn't exist and regard it as impossible.

1 Corinthians 4:5 (AMP)

So do not go on passing judgment before the appointed time, but wait until the Lord comes, for He will both bring to light the [secret] things that are hidden in darkness and disclose the motives of the hearts. Then each one's praise will come from God.

1 Corinthians 4:5 (MSG)

So don't get ahead of the Master and jump to conclusions with your judgments before all the evidence is in. When he comes, he will bring out in the open and place in evidence all kinds of things we never even dreamed of—inner motives and purposes and prayers. Only then will any one of us get to hear the "Well done!" of God.

Isaiah 48:6 (AMP)
"You have heard [these things foretold]; look at all this [that has been fulfilled]. And you, will you not declare it? I proclaim to you [specific] new things from this time, Even [a]hidden things which you have not known.

Isaiah 48:6 (MSG)
I have a lot more to tell you, things you never knew existed. This isn't a variation on the same r guess or dream up. When you hear this you won't be able to say, 'I knew that all along.'

Deuteronomy 29:29 (AMP)
"The secret things belong to the Lord our God, but the things which are revealed and disclosed belong to us and to our children forever, so that we may do all of the words of this law.

God, our God, will take care of the hidden things but the revealed things are our business. It's up to us and our children to attend to all the terms in this Revelation.

The disparity between God and science, technology, or any other earthly solution lies in their approach: they are reactive, whereas God is proactive. God doesn't wait for problems to arise before looking for a solution. Knowing that the Lamb was slain before the foundation of the world validates that God has made provision for a solution to every form of impossibility we will ever face in this world. We do not have to be afraid, worry, or be frustrated ever again for the rest of our lives. All we need is to trust and ask God for supernatural illumination whenever we face impossible situations or limitations, and we will break all limits by His grace.

We should see all impossible problems as opportunities to discover the pre-existing solution anytime we face it. Whenever we encounter impossible problems, we should view them as opportunities to uncover the pre-existing solution. That implies we should perceive impossibilities as possibilities waiting to be uncovered. This mindset of viewing impossibilities as opportunities or possibilities has the potential to alleviate frustration, anxiety, worry, confusion, and all other factors that may contribute to depression, thereby reducing suicide rates significantly.

This mindset will also foster motivation for problem-solving and enhance our ability to confront and overcome challenges, rather than allowing them to defeat us or hinder our progress in life.

Notes

CHAPTER 3

THE DANGER OF EXCUSES

Excuses are the enemy of progress. Regardless of how reasonable they seem when presented, how real they appear, how much sense they make, or how convincing they sound. Excuses are merely a deceptive illusion crafted to rob us of our dreams, extinguish our visions, derail our destiny, sabotage our chances, divert us from our God-ordained opportunities, and eliminate possibilities.

Excuses show up as mountains or obstacles on our way to victory. They are the reasons we classify an issue as impossible. They are strategically and intentionally designed by the devil to discourage us from doing what is needed to challenge and defeat the impossible.

Excuses serve as a self-inflicted disqualifier, preventing us from rightfully claiming what belongs to us. They are deceptive lies or narratives concocted by the devil, accepted as legitimate reasons for our failure, convincing us that we cannot meet the requirements necessary for success in various aspects of life. Excuses have the potential to destroy our motivation and deter us from pursuing our God-given visions. However, for those who discern their true nature, excuses can be seen as hidden treasure and transformative blessings in disguise.

Like the giants in the promised land, excuses are not intended to halt our progress but rather to motivate us. Excuses are the identity cards of people with a grasshopper mentality or identify individuals with a defeatist mentality. Excuses are lies of the devil sold to those foolish enough to buy them, sluggard's self-accepted limitations, loser's comfort zone used by people who are not willing to pay the price, an elastic limit or breaking point set for slackers and provide a comfortable refuge for those unwilling to exert effort. Excuses represent self-imposed limitations and serve as a crutch for those unwilling to strive for greatness. They are the devil's primary weapon of discouragement, aimed at thwarting our potential and hindering our progress.

Finally, your excuses are your blindside. They reveal areas of untapped potential and highlight areas in need of improvement. You cannot physically see their consequences or what you stand to miss immediately. We require divine illumination and a broader vision to discover their true mission and expose their true color. Excuses are fueled by misconceptions, proven or unproven facts that we have subscribed to, unfounded or wrong conclusions drawn from faulty mechanisms, negative experiences, personal weaknesses, massively corrupt culture we have imbibed, unfavorable laws; loose thoughts; false emotions and impulses; unfounded sophisticated arguments; myopic warped philosophies and societal influences. They erect barriers against the true knowledge of God, distorting our perception and hindering our growth. Thus, it's crucial to confront excuses with wisdom, discernment, and a steadfast commitment to overcome them, embracing a mindset of growth and resilience in the face of adversity. Only by recognizing their true nature can we overcome excuses and realize our full potential.

THIRTY-EIGHT YEARS OF EXCUSES

There was a paralyzed man who had been in the same spot for thirty-eight years, stagnant because he failed to make efforts to progress in life. He blamed his condition on his position. Jesus met him and asked him if he wanted to be healed so that he could make progress. He started using his condition to make excuses for his past failure as if Jesus did not know this before asking him that question. He also said he didn't have a man to help him, which was the same excuse that Mary had but didn't stop her from obtaining the promise of God.

John 5:2-9 (MSG)

2-6. Soon another Feast came around and Jesus was back in Jerusalem. Near the Sheep Gate in Jerusalem, there was a pool, in Hebrew called Bethesda, with five alcoves. Hundreds of sick people—blind, crippled, paralyzed—were in these alcoves. One man had been an invalid there for thirty-eight years. When Jesus saw him stretched out by the pool and knew how long he had been there, he said, "Do you want to get well?" 7. The sick man said, "Sir, when the water is stirred,I don't have anybody to put me in the pool. By the time I get there, somebody else is already in." 8-9. Jesus said, "Get up, take your bedroll, and start walking." The man was healed on the spot. He picked up his bedroll and walked off.

Looking at this story critically, he was not the only impotent man in that position. Some of them had made desperate efforts to obtain their healing and had left him in the same spot. Whenever I consider his circumstances and imagine myself in his shoes, I realize that if I had just one opportunity to improve my life, I would do whatever it took to seize it. While some people face terminal medical diagnoses with no recourse to salvage their situation, this man was not without options. Even if it meant crawling inch by inch to position myself to enter the pool first, I would have done so without hesitation. I might have even considered remaining in the pool, ensuring that the angel found me there. The question to ask is how did he do the other things that helped him to survive for thirty-eight years? He must have been eating and bathing or else he would have died in that same spot of hunger or sickness. How was he pooping? He couldn't have been pooping on the same spot either. He had help for everything except the main thing with the potential to change his life for good.

This can be likened to what happened during the coronavirus pandemic. People could go to every other place (gas station, grocery store, mall, doctor's office, etc) but wouldn't attend church due to the fear of the coronavirus. My conclusion is that he was complacent and he got used to the easy advantage that his condition had earned him. The handouts and pity he received prevented him from striving to improve his situation. There was no indication in his response to Jesus that he desired to change his position; he had become accustomed to that lifestyle and resigned himself to being an invalid.

However, Jesus disregarded all of his excuses and proceeded to heal him, despite his resistance. Jesus was demonstrating that there was at least one option the man had not explored, one that could have made all the difference. The option was Jesus Christ! He probably would have heard the news of the exploits of Jesus. The pool option was a once-in-a-year opportunity while the Jesus' option was an everyday opportunity in that season. The summary of this story is that he remained in the same spot for thirty-eight years. Can you imagine how many things he had missed in life?

DEVIL'S STRATEGIC WEAPON

John 10:10 (AMP)

The thief comes only in order to steal and kill and destroy. I came that they may have and enjoy life, and have it in abundance [to the full, till it overflows].

The Devil's main target is the promises of God that are made available for the children of God. Excuses are the devil's strategic weapon that he uses to steal our motivation to believe and do what it takes to obtain the promises of God given to us. Excuses are like weapons aimed at destroying our dreams, ultimately thwarting our chances of achieving them. Excuses will hold us in the same spot for as long as we allow them to hold us hostage.

Many of us find ourselves in a similar position as the man by the pool, using our circumstances or what we lack as excuses for not fulfilling our God-given dreams or for not breaking free from a satanic predicament. Some individuals claim they are unable to further their education or improve their lives due to a lack of domestic support, assistance, or resources. Others cite the demands of parenting as a reason for not serving God effectively. Many resort to using their busy schedules or other obligations as excuses. However, it's crucial to recognize that every time we make excuses, we open ourselves up to the thief's trap, risking the loss of something invaluable.

Excuses are the reasons we concoct in our minds for why we cannot achieve God's given dream. People often use their accent, lack of influence, bad luck, the complexity or difficulty of a problem, poor credit, shyness, stage fright, past failures, fears, immigration status, race, gender, educational barriers, age, scientific laws, financial limitations, time constraints, seasonality, death or irreversibility, medical constraints, and physiological background as excuses for why they cannot progress and make a difference in life.

Sometimes we hear statements like, "The reason I have developed sexually deviant behaviors or engage in a promiscuous lifestyle is because I was sexually abused when I was young." Some blame their failure on the fact that their parents abandoned them and they had to live in the foster care system. Some say they are in prison because they had no father figure and some blame going back to prison on the fact that society will not accept them. Some use racism as an excuse for not trying hard to succeed. Some blame their addiction on everything you can possibly think of. Spouses blame one another's attitude for their marital crisis or failure. Older single ladies or men use age, looks, or past disappointment as excuses for why they have stopped looking forward to the possibility of getting married and they just mess around with anyone available. Some blame their sex, race, or immigration status as the primary disqualifier that has exempted them from all great opportunities.

Some individuals have lost hope and no longer trust in God's plan for their own children due to their irreversible medical diagnosis. With advancing age, any remaining hope seems to have dwindled away. Some even think that their business, career, and everything else has been damaged beyond repair. Others chose suicide as an option because they believed that no one cared or loved them enough for them to continue to stay alive.

It's important to note that we are not attempting to trivialize or diminish the profound impact and trauma of such incidents. We acknowledge the significant challenges they present. However, our message is one of hope and empowerment: that despite the obstacles, there is a way forward, and these challenges do not have to limit our chances or dictate the course of our lives. With right attitude, wisdom, perseverance, support, and determination, we can overcome adversity and chart a path to healing and success.

BREAKING NEWS - NO EXCUSE IS TENABLE

All excuses are defeatable! There are people who have succeeded, overcome and made a difference in life in spite of all the excuses mentioned above. Wherever there is a will, there is a way. If you are willing and obedient, the Bible says you will eat the good of the land. No excuse is acceptable under heaven. No excuse is powerful enough to stop you from being productive as designed by God.

We are richly blessed and highly favored and we are too loaded to be defeated by any excuse from the pit of hell. See the way the scripture put it;

Romans 1:20 (NKJV)
For the invisible things of him from the creation of the world are clearly seen, being understood by the things that are made, even his eternal power and Godhead; so that they are ***without excuse***

This passage is saying that the testimonies of all impossible situations that have been made possible by God's eternal power captured in the scripture as stories were packaged for us to understand how spiritual processes and principles work. It continues to say that **God is the Headmaster not your excuses.** Therefore, no excuse is tenable for failure!

Mark 11:12-14;21-23 (MSG)
As they left Bethany the next day, he was hungry. Off in the distance, he saw a fig tree in full leaf. He came up to it expecting to find something for breakfast but found nothing but fig leaves. (It wasn't yet the season for figs.) He addressed the tree: "No one is going to eat fruit from you again—ever!" And his disciples overheard him.

20-21 In the morning, walking along the road, they saw the fig tree, shriveled to a dry stick. Peter, remembering what had happened the previous day, said to him, "Rabbi, look—the fig tree you cursed is shriveled up!"

22-23 Jesus was matter-of-fact: "Embrace this God-life. Really embrace it, and nothing will be too much for you. This mountain, for instance: Just say, 'Go jump in the lake'—no shuffling or hemming and hawing—and it's as good as done That's why I urge you to pray for absolutely everything, ranging from small to large. Include everything as you embrace this God-life, and you'll get God's everything.

This tree had a valid excuse at the time but it was not accepted by Jesus. Jesus would never demand from you what you can't produce. He will not demand from you what He has not put in you. In the Bible, trees are metaphors for human beings in Christ. In some places, He said we shall be like trees planted by the rivers of water that produce fruit in and out of season. We are planted by the rivers. Our own river is the Word of God (Ephesians 5:26). The implication of this analogy is that, If we are planted by the river, that means we are immune to drought and consequently, we are configured with the capacity to produce extraordinary results in and out of season.

Jesus himself performed a miracle in the marriage at Cana of Galilee before his time to launch his ministry. He did not use the fact as an excuse not to make a difference in that marriage ceremony. Jesus is not a task master. If Jesus did not accept the excuse of the fig tree, understand that it is because He had programmed the tree with the ability to produce fruit in and out of season, that was why the fig tree was punished for using the season as an excuse for not fulfilling its divine assignment or meeting divine expectation.

Your reading this book testifies to the truth in my life that excuse is a thief of opportunity. I have been trying to write a book for the past five years and have not succeeded till now. I have blamed it on situations and circumstances that prevented me from writing it. From lack of inspiration to being busy, not having enough time to write, demands of the church, family obligations, work, and business responsibilities. The reality is that my own lack of determination to pay the price has prevented me from writing it. I shifted blame onto others and external circumstances, refusing to take responsibility for my actions.

It's important to note that accepting blame or taking responsibility should not stem from a place of regret, defeat, or accusation. It is from a standpoint of acknowledging responsibility for one's negative attitude and being motivated to overcome all excuses on the path to fulfillment. **Excuses do not have more power than the ones we give them.** Excuses cannot stop you until you accept to be stopped. Every time you make excuses for your shortcomings you are empowering it to stop you from succeeding in the areas you ought to be successful.

Excuses are a sign that you have accepted defeat or settled for the status quo, and you do not want to take responsibility for your actions, improve or change so that your situation can also change. **Greatness is exclusively reserved for those who refuse to be enslaved by excuses or succumb to the tyranny of excuse-making.**

Notes

CHAPTER 4

THE GOD FACTOR

Luke 1:37 (KJV)
For with God nothing shall be impossible.

If Paul plants, and Apollos waters, ultimately, it is God who determines the quality and outcome of the results. God's factor is an indispensable requirement for anyone that wants to experience an extraordinary life. In Luke 1:34, Mary questioned the angel about the feasibility of how what she was told would manifest as a physical reality. The verse above captures the angel's response. The angel informed her that the task she perceived as impossible could only be achieved by God through the assistance of the Holy Spirit and the power of the Most High.

She was assured that nothing is impossible with God. This implies that when God permits you to encounter a situation that seems humanly impossible, you should not be intimidated by the probability of its execution. It is a job exclusively reserved for Him alone to perform. He only wants to use you for His glory. The implication is that you are just a specimen to be used while He is the one with the capacity to perform the miracle.

The power of the Highest means the highest order of power. This type of power is exclusive to God. All power belongs to God! It is the supreme power that transcends all others. This divine power, wielded by God, is the force behind miraculous interventions. Consequently, it is this inherent superiority of God's power that provides the foundation upon which God's power continually outshines any other force responsible for the problem at hand. Ultimately, all power emanates from God, underscoring His sovereignty and omnipotence.

Psalms 62:11 (NKJV)
God has spoken once, twice I have heard this: That power belongs to God.

Matthew 28:18 (AMP)
Jesus came up and said to them, "All authority (all power of absolute rule) in heaven and on earth has been given to Me.

That is why we need to defer to God in impossible situations. God does not give us promises that we are able to accomplish by ourselves. If He is the one that promised us then He is the only one that has the capacity to fulfill it.

1 Thessalonians 5:24 (KJV)
Faithful is he that calleth you, who also will do it.

The One who called you is completely dependable. If He said it, He would do it! He doesn't promise what He cannot do. One of the attributes of God is immutability, which is the fact that He cannot lie. Even if He chooses to lie, His nature will not allow it. Hence whatever He promised in His Word is an insight into what He has the capacity to do.

The way God works is that there are laws He has set in place that controls how everything He created is expected to function on earth. He has submitted Himself voluntarily to the terms and conditions of these laws in order to protect His integrity. By Law, God cannot physically come down to the earth to do whatever needs to be done on the earth by Himself or He will be violating His own law.

The moment He commanded man to have dominion on the earth, it became the law and placed the sole responsibility of executing His plan on the earth with man. Therefore, it is illegal for Him to do anything on earth without the approval or cooperation of mankind. Therefore, God works through humans to demonstrate His power. That's why the Bible says we can do all things through Christ who strengthens us. However, ultimately, He remains the source and owner of that power.

SPIRITUAL ASPECT VS PHYSICAL ASPECT

God is not a magician but a miracle worker. The distinction between miracles and magic lies in the collaborative process between God and man. Miracles entail human action in the physical realm alongside divine intervention in the supernatural. Conversely, magic presents as a sudden event devoid of process or cooperation, expecting superficial outcomes without human involvement

Therefore, any time God wants to execute His plan on earth, He has to recruit a man that will do the required physical work. That is why the bible says that except God builds a house in the spirit, anyone that tries to build it physically is wasting his time.

Based on this, the spiritual becomes the mother of the physical. Everything on earth that does not proceed from the realm of the spirit by God remains impossible. That means that things that are currently impossible will remain impossible until God and heaven get involved. This is called divine intervention.

Once the God of heaven, the custodian of the highest level of power, gets involved, the case is settled. You don't need Him to get involved in things you can do for yourself, you only need to get His approval. But you need Him to get involved in things you cannot get yourself out of or fix by yourself. He initiates the action from heaven and relies on your actions to trigger the manifestation of His initiated action on earth. He depends on you to do the simple part while He does the complex part.

Anytime you are asking questions like "How shall this be" and you cannot rationalize the possibility of a resolution from every angle you look at it, know that you are not minding your business. You are poking your nose into God's business. If it is your business, you will know the "HOW". If it is His business, you will never know "HOW". When you don't know the "HOW", then you know it is His business. One thing I can be sure of is that He is God all by Himself and He can always handle His business all by Himself. He doesn't need you to help Him out. He needs you to mind your business.

That is where the formula for the faith that produces miracles is derived from. We will discuss this in much detail in the next chapter.

For example, the role of Moses at the Red Sea when the children of Israel had to cross over to the other side was to stretch forth the rod for the Red Sea to part. Stretching out the rod over the sea is like speaking the Word or acting on the Word. Jesus is the Rod and Stem of Jesse as well as the Word and the Wisdom of God. What Moses did in his day is equal to what God expects us to do in our day. The action that triggered the east wind to blow and part the Red Sea creating a pathway of dry land within the sea is inexplicable because it was on God to do it.

His judgments are unsearchable and His ways are past finding out. Therefore, whenever you can't figure out your way, or there is no way under heaven available for you to fix it, just know that that's when you need to get God involved.

Wherever there is a "WILL", there is a way! That's God's specialty, doing the impossible! The WILL here is not just limited to your willpower but also His "WILL", that is, His "WORD". This means that whatever His Word covers, there is a way! There is always a way with God!

With God nothing is impossible! God is the only one who can do the impossible and make a way where there is no way.

Job 5:9 (NKJV)
Who does great and unsearchable things, Marvelous things without number?

Romans 11:33 (AMP)
Oh, the depth of the riches and wisdom and knowledge of God! How unsearchable are His judgments and decisions and how unfathomable and untraceable are His ways!

Have you ever encountered anything as extravagant as the generosity of God, or as profound as His wisdom? It is way over our heads. We'll never figure it out.

The angel's answer to Mary indicates that regardless of how you feel about the impossibility of the situation, with God it is possible. It may be impossible with science and technology but it is a simple thing with God. The Bible says that what is impossible with men is possible with God.

THE DISTINCTION OF THE GOD FACTOR

Genesis 39:2-3 (AMP)

2. The Lord was with Joseph, and he [even though a slave] became a successful and prosperous man; and he was in the house of his master, the Egyptian.

3. Now his master saw that the Lord was with him and that the Lord caused all that he did to prosper (succeed) in his hand.

Only the God that I serve can turn a slave to the second in command of the King of the greatest nation on earth. If this God is with us, nothing can work against us or no one can win against us.

With God, Jesus and Peter defied the law of buoyancy to walk on water. With God, Jesus defied the law of death to raise up the dead Lazarus who had been in the grave for four days. Remember, the Bible says, "It is given for man to die once, after which there is judgment." However, when the God Factor is involved in any situation, lower laws must always yield to God's higher laws. With God, Jesus and Elijah defied the law of gravity. They went up and never came down. With God, Peter defied the law of fishery that restricted professional fishing to night time. With God, you can defy any law or constitution. There is no limit to what anyone can accomplish with God.

In summary, I can equally let you know that with God you can beat cancer or any terminal disease at any stage. You can come out of any amount of debt like the widow whose husband left her bankrupt. You can beat inflation and recession as Isaac did. With God, like Esther, you can defy immigration laws and become the queen or king of any kingdom the soles of your feet touch. With God, you can have a baby without a womb, or non-functional reproductive organs like Sarah and Abraham. With God, you can come out of prison without being affected by your prison record just like Joseph or the three Hebrew boys. Like Ruth, it is possible to find your dream husband or wife at any age, with God. With God, it is possible to succeed in life despite growing up in a foster home. With God, it is possible to overcome abuse or addiction of any kind. No case is closed with God and your case can never be over with Him.

Notes

CHAPTER 5

THE YOU FACTOR

One of the most important things everyone needs to embrace after becoming born again is self-recognition, self-rediscovery, and self- reinvention.

This entails knowing who you are, recognizing your potential in relation to your current circumstances, and understanding the required evolution - growth and development needed to reach your destination. Knowing who you are will help you discover your potential and divine assignment. Your potential is a blend of what you possess and what you can achieve, including abilities you may not yet be aware of.

Until you discover your true identity, there is a significant risk of living a life that does not align with who you truly are. This can lead to ongoing frustration and difficulty in realizing your full potential and destiny. There will always be a vacuum left in you that cannot be filled with anything else but your divine assignment. Everything God has deposited in you will continue to cry out internally for expression until you become what you are created to be.

NO EXPERIENCE IS WASTED

There exists a direct correlation between every challenge you have faced or will face in life and your divine purpose. That is why everything you have gone through in life or will go through in life revolves around your purpose.

Moses was in exile in the wilderness for forty years because he would need the experience to lead the children of Israel out of Egypt through the wilderness to the promised land. The number of years He spent in exile in the wilderness actually also matched the exact number of years the children of Israel wandered in the wilderness before getting to the promised land.

David also had to learn how to rule as a king over the sheep before he was entrusted with human beings. The experience he had fighting and defeating the lion and the bear in the wilderness gave him the confidence he used to confront and defeat Goliath.

Joseph had to acquire the skills of empathetic leadership in handling slaves and prisoners, as well as effectively managing his boss's business empire and the prison unit. Only then did God entrust him with the destiny of a nation. The tougher the hardship for Joseph, the closer he was to his breakthrough.

The common factor between all the experiences detailed above is God's unconditional love orchestrating the purpose of these experiences.

The first thing we need to embrace as we navigate through life's experiences is that God loves us unconditionally and we are His cherished children. Therefore, it's crucial to always remember that God has your best interests at heart, no matter how dire the situation may seem.

1 John 3:1-2 (KJV)

Behold, what manner of love the Father hath bestowed upon us, that we should be called the sons of God: therefore the world knoweth us not, because it knew him not.

Beloved, now are we the sons of God, and it doth not yet appear what we shall be: but we know that, when he shall appear, we shall be like him; for we shall see him as he is.

1 John 3:1-2 (MSG)

What marvelous love the Father has extended to us! Just look at it—we're called children of God! That's who we really are. But that's also why the world doesn't recognize us or take us seriously because it has no idea who he is or what he's up to.
2-3 But friends, that's exactly who we are: children of God. And that's only the beginning. Who knows how we'll end up! What we know is that when Christ is openly revealed, we'll see him—and in seeing him, become like him.

1 John 3:1-2 (MSG)

See what an incredible quality of love the Father has shown to us, that we would [be permitted to] be named and called and counted the children of God! And so we are! For this reason, the world does not know us, because it did not know Him. 2 Beloved, we are [even here and] now children of God, and it is not yet made clear what we will be [after His coming]. We know that when He comes and is revealed, we will [as His children] be like Him because we will see Him just as He is [in all His glory].

God's love towards you is always the game changer. It is unconditional and does not discriminate. It is not partial or racially inclined.

A LOVING GOD

Most of the time, people attribute their negative experiences or adversity to being punishment for something they have done wrong. Unknown to them, God never punishes us with evil. Who will in his right mind punish his child with death or catastrophe? He only allows it whenever He wants to showcase His power and stretch our faith.

However, God may sometimes exhibit some tough aspects of this love towards us whenever He is bent on keeping us in the direction of the blessing. He also allows it whenever it is going to work for our good. Implying our problems serve a purpose that may only be fully understood at the conclusion of the process. Yet, in hindsight, we will come to realize that God always had our best interests at heart and may have permitted us to endure it for our own benefit. God is not a taskmaster eagerly awaiting our mistakes so He can pounce on us; rather, He is a loving and compassionate Father. He is a loving God who constantly watches over us and gently guides us to overcome our weaknesses. He made His strength perfect in our weaknesses, and also made His grace available for us to cover our weaknesses. He is always there with and for us to pick us up if we fall.

Before I grasped this tender, loving aspect of Him, I often perceived God as punishing me whenever something negative occurred in my life. I would be so discouraged and unable to approach Him for help. I held a mindset that believed enduring prolonged suffering and serving punishment was necessary for me to earn God's sympathy before I could approach Him and seek His forgiveness. So, I endured in silence, continuing to suffer for as long as possible, assuming that eventually, He would show me mercy.

FAVOR, GRACE AND MERCY

The revelation of the power of favor, grace, and mercy was my game-changer. This shifted the dynamics of my relationship with Him. I realized that His grace is an undeserved favor that grants me what I do not merit

That means God does not do good to me because I am a good person. He always does good because by nature He cannot do any evil, even if He wanted to do it, He is constantly good. Therefore, regardless of what I do, His constant disposition towards me would be to do me good. I also discovered that it is by His mercy that we have not been consumed.

Mercy therefore, is God's attribute that refrains from giving us what we deserve in response to our actions. Instead, He uses His goodness to motivate us to become a better person. A great example is the woman that was caught in the act of adultery (John 8:11). Instead of being stoned to death, she was pardoned, given another chance and asked not to sin any more. Mercy is an undeserved pardon. Just as He demonstrated with the prodigal son.

Luke 15:17- 32 (MSG)

17-20 "That brought him to his senses. He said, 'All those farmhands working for my father sit down to three meals a day, and here I am starving to death. I'm going back to my father. I'll say to him, Father, I've sinned against God, I've sinned before you; I don't deserve to be called your son. Take me on as a hired hand.' He got right up and went home to his father.

20-21 "When he was still a long way off, his father saw him. His heart pounding, he ran out, embraced him, and kissed him. The son started his speech: 'Father, I've sinned against God, I've sinned before you; I don't deserve to be called your son ever again.'

22-24 "But the father wasn't listening. He was calling to the servants, 'Quick. Bring a clean set of clothes and dress him. Put the family ring on his finger and sandals on his feet. Then get a prize-winning heifer and roast it. We're going to feast! We're going to have a wonderful time! My son is here—given up for dead and now alive! Given up for lost and now found!' And they began to have a wonderful time.

25-27 "All this time his older son was out in the field. When the day's work was done he came in. As he approached the house, he heard the music and dancing. Calling over one of the houseboys, he asked what was going on. He told him, 'Your brother came home. Your father has ordered a feast—barbecued beef!—because he has him home safe and sound.'

28-30 "The older brother stomped off in an angry sulk and refused to join in. His father came out and tried to talk to him, but he wouldn't listen. The son said, 'Look how many years I've stayed here serving you, never giving you one moment of grief, but have you ever thrown a party for me and my friends? Then this son of yours who has thrown away your money on whores shows up and you go all out with a feast!'

31-32 "His father said, 'Son, you don't understand. You're with me all the time, and everything that is mine is yours—but this is a wonderful time, and we had to celebrate. This brother of yours was dead, and he's alive! He was lost, and he's found!'"

This prodigal son was just like me. He did not go back home on time. He did not understand the concept of grace and mercy. God's mercy is everlasting! Mercy serves as God's divine strategy to counteract any legal ground the devil may claim against us, preventing him from leveraging it to demand justice for our wrongdoings. This helps to protect us from being isolated from God and trapped in perpetual bondage. Mercy is our safety net! Mercy is the divine loophole embedded in God's constitution that we can always rely on whenever we make mistakes. God already knows that we are not immune to mistakes. God recognizes that we are a work in progress and does not want the devil to have any legal grounds to sabotage our growth towards perfection.

Grace is defined as undeserved favor. Grace was proactively designed by God to provide us with opportunities we do not deserve, despite the mistakes we may make. However, if we were not consumed because of His mercy, that means that mercy is our insurance coverage against the evil judgment that we deserved.

Grace then becomes our divine qualifier for the good we don't deserve while mercy is our divine exemption from the punishment we deserve. Therefore, the **Mercy and Grace Combo** creates a win-win opportunity for us through the unfeigned love of God.

DINING WITH PIGS

As illustrated in the parable of the prodigal son, his story serves as a symbolic representation of the foolishness we find ourselves in when we believe we have irreparably damaged our relationship with God. Pigs according to the scripture are a metaphor for non-believers. In one of the many parables of Jesus Christ, He said, "Cast not your pearls before the swine because they will trample upon it". This means there are things the unbeliever can never value because such things can only be spiritually discerned. By joining with the pigs and eating their food, it metaphorically signifies that he descended to the level of unbelievers, competing for what was available to them. Eating with the pigs is symbolic of limitation, being restricted to what was only made available on earth. It is akin to crumbs from the children's bread that fall from the table.

Eating with pigs could mean that we are not eating from the heavenly table. An unbeliever has been alienated from the heavenly table thereby experiences similar restrictions in life. Unbelievers are constrained to consume only what is available in the natural realm. This is what the Bible refers to as crumbs that fall from the table.

Pigs are not granted access to shop in the marketplace of the supernatural, where impossible items are displayed.

The limitations of their mindset are defined by the limits imposed by science, medicine, and technology. They are at the mercy of medicine for their health recovery; they are at mercy of science and technology for solutions to their problems. Anytime medicine, science, and technology are stranded, they are also equally stranded. This was what the life of the prodigal son had degenerated into.

The unfortunate aspect is that the degeneration was self-inflicted due to a lack of knowledge and willful disobedience. When the prodigal son came to his senses, he realized that the kingdom he and his Father had been a part of was a realm of limitless possibilities. He leveraged the concept of the provision of grace and mercy and decided to throw himself at the mercy of His father. The end result was an amazing display of the Father's unconditional love. He was not only forgiven and celebrated but he was also restored to his state of authority as if he had done nothing wrong!

GOD'S INVESTMENT

God loves you unconditionally! If He willingly chose to die for you when you were worthless, helpless, and without the strength to save yourself, what else could possibly come between you and Him after you have accepted Him as your

Lord and personal savior? You are His divine real estate investment! He cannot afford to let His investment go down the drain. You are His favorite child – there is nothing you can do wrong for Him to stop loving you.

WHO YOU ARE

According to 1 John 3:2, "now are we the children of God!" Therefore, this means that you are His child NOW!! Not when you start doing the right things. You are His favorite child NOW!, on your way to doing the right things!! You are not a nobody now, you are somebody NOW! You are not a nonentity; you are the apple of His eyes NOW! You are not a loser, you are a winner NOW! You are not a failure, you are a success NOW! You are not dumb, You are smart because you have the mind of Christ, a sound mind NOW! You are not a crackhead, or a pimp, neither are you ugly; you are fearfully and wonderfully made. You are not a totality of what anyone can see now! You are an object of evolution, an evolution of divinity through the nature of Christ.

Everything that is in Christ Jesus is programmed to find expression through you. 1 John 3:2 further says that "when Christ is openly revealed, we'll see him—and in seeing him, become like him." The world can never define us correctly until they know Him. Regardless of what is currently evident in us physically, what is in Christ Jesus will ultimately prevail over it in due time. As you walk with Him and adhere to His Word, every aspect of your being will gradually transform to reflect His character and align with what He has declared in His Word. Therefore, everything He said you are, is what you have been scheduled to potentially become by His grace.

LIVE IN THE NOW

You don't have to wait for the physical manifestation of this truth before you start acting like it. You are a king and a priest NOW! not a servant. You are above and not beneath NOW! You are rich and wealthy NOW! because He has already paid the price in full by becoming poor that you might become rich. His blessing makes you rich and adds no sorrow NOW! You are not barren, you are fruitful NOW!

You are healthy and not a sickler NOW! He took your infirmities and by His stripes, you were healed. You will lend to nations, you are not a borrower NOW! You are completely free from generational curses NOW! not in any way locked down; You are a winner and not a loser NOW! You are somebody NOW! not a nobody. You are married NOW! and not a disadvantaged single parent. You are beautiful NOW! you are fearfully and wonderfully made. You have a job NOW! not jobless. Your marriage is bubbling NOW! two are better than one; Marriage is an initiation into a good life and good times. You are not divorced NOW! whatsoever the Lord has joined together let no man put asunder.

You are more than a conqueror and have overcome the world. You are a celebrity and not a nonentity. You are the light of the world, a city set on a hill that cannot be hidden. You have hidden riches of secret places. They that seek God will not lack any good thing.

Jesus is the firstborn and we are his blood brothers. We are created like God, we have every attribute that God has. Like Father like Son; We are joint heirs with Christ. We have the nature of God; we shall manifest His glory.

You are blessed and highly favored! You are too loaded to fail, too gifted to be wasted, too powerful to be ignored, and too valuable to be unproductive. Everything that is in God is also already in you NOW, you can do everything that God can do, so whatever cannot stop or limit God cannot stop or limit you.

Until you discover your self-worth, you will continue to settle for less, suffer insecurity, and low self-esteem, contemplate suicide, back off impossible challenges and not attempt great things. Statements like "I am not good enough"; "it's out of my league"; "I don't have what it takes"; " I am not cut out for this", and "why is this happening to me", are the vocabulary of such people.

Here is the deal, if you shop only in the marketplace of possibilities and avoid impossibilities, you would have missed out on greatness and you may never stand out. You will underutilize the purpose of grace - (2 Cor 6:1) says "Receive not His grace in vain as workers together with God". He works in you both to will and to do! He works through you to accomplish impossibilities. Understanding and embracing the new creation reality of the YOU factor in Christ Jesus will help you to overcome the self-imposed limitations placed on you through ignorance. This will help you to leverage every grace that God has made available for you to do the impossible in life.

Notes

CHAPTER 6

THE HOLY GHOST FACTOR

Zechariah 4:6-9 (AMP)

Then he said to me, "This [continuous supply of oil] is the word of the Lord to Zerubbabel [prince of Judah], saying, 'Not by might, nor by power, but by My Spirit [of whom the oil is a symbol],' says the Lord of hosts.
7 'What are you, O great mountain [of obstacles]? Before Zerubbabel [who will rebuild the temple] you will become a plain (insignificant)!
And he will bring out the capstone [of the new temple] with loud shouts of "Grace, grace to it!"'"
8 Also the word of the Lord came to me, saying,
9 "The hands of Zerubbabel have laid the foundations of this house, and his hands will finish it. Then you will know (recognize, understand fully) that the Lord of hosts has sent me [as His messenger] to you.

The Holy Spirit is the X-factor in every extraordinary result performed on earth since the transition of power from Jesus to Him. Jesus' Era has passed; He completed His assignment and ended his Era through His death and His resurrection. He himself said "It is finished" on the cross of Calvary. This is now the Holy Ghost Era. Whatever the Trinity wants to do now in this era on earth is done through the help of the Holy Spirit. That is why He is called the Helper. He is constituted to help us to accomplish the impossible.

1 Samuel 2:9 (KJV)
He will keep the feet of his saints, and the wicked shall be silent in darkness; for ***by strength shall no man prevail.***

It takes supernatural power to make impossibility possible. Such power can only be facilitated by the Holy Spirit. God is a great God, and He alone does great and wondrous things. However, in this dispensation, He does it through the help of the Holy Spirit that dwells in us.

God will never give you a dream you can achieve all by yourself.

God depends on man to accomplish His great purpose on earth because He has handed over the authority and dominion on earth to man. However, this authority is a delegated authority that is solely dependent on the power of God. Therefore, mankind requires the assistance of the Holy Spirit to tap into the power that supports the authority and dominion bestowed upon us by God, enabling us to achieve tasks that are humanly impossible but commissioned by God.

Zechariah 4:6 (KJV)
Then he answered and spake unto me, saying, This is the word of the LORD unto Zerubbabel, saying, Not by might, nor by power, but by my spirit, saith the LORD of hosts.

That is why in His word He said "Faithful is He that called you, who will also do it".(1 Thess 5:24) This means the one who recruited you for the impossible mission is the one who is solely responsible to do the complex part and He is faithful to play His part without fail.

For example, when God wanted to give birth to greatness on earth, He recruited Mary for the mission.

Luke 1:30-31; 34-37; 41-45 (KJV)
30 And the angel said unto her, Fear not, Mary: for thou hast found favor with God.
31 And, behold, thou shalt conceive in thy womb, and bring forth a son, and shalt call his name JESUS.
34 Then said Mary unto the angel, How shall this be, seeing I know not a man?
35 And the angel answered and said unto her, The Holy Ghost shall come upon thee, and the power of the Highest shall overshadow thee: therefore also that holy thing which shall be born of thee shall be called the Son of God.
45 And blessed is she that believed: for there shall be a performance of those things which were told her from the Lord.

In this passage, Mary asked the angel an interesting question that centers on trying to know how that seeming impossibility could become possible. The angel used a puzzle to answer her question. This puzzle showed where the **Holy Ghost, the power of God, God himself** and faith fit into the equation of unlimited possibilities.

Here is the content of the puzzle; "The **HOLY GHOST** shall come upon you"; "the **POWER** of the Highest shall overshadow you"; "WITH GOD, nothing shall be impossible"; "behold, thy cousin Elisabeth, she hath also conceived a son in her old age: and this is the sixth month with her, who was called barren" and "blessed is she that **BELIEVED:** for there shall be a performance of those things which were told her from the Lord".

If we have to arrange this puzzle in sequential order, the first thing we will realize is that all things are possible with GOD. That means the side you align with determines the difference between what will be possible and what will remain impossible. Standing with God is what turns impossibility into possibility. God fulfills His promises when we believe and align ourselves with Him. The second thing we will realize is what the angel told Mary about the Holy Spirit. And the angel answered and said unto her, "The HOLY GHOST shall come upon thee, and the POWER OF THE HIGHEST shall overshadow thee" This means that the process of transforming impossibility to possibility by God is routed through the assistance of the Holy Spirit and the power of the highest, that is, the highest order of power.

The Holy Spirit comes upon you to connect you with His power. He uses the highest order of power to overshadow any impossible situation. This power is released and transmitted by the Holy Spirit to assist humanity in accomplishing impossible tasks when we have faith. Therefore, the Holy Spirit must be involved in anything that appears impossible to pave the way for the highest level of power to intervene and make it possible.

However, in Amos 3:3 the Bible says "Can two walk together except they agree?" Walking with God successfully requires alignment with His word and principles. Faith is essentially walking in agreement with God, choosing to take side with His truth over worldly perceptions or circumstances. This necessitates a willingness to walk by faith, not by sight, and to prioritize God's Word above all else. Whatever contradicts God's promises holds no weight as long as it does not align with what God says. Only God's Word holds true significance. By applying God's Word with unwavering faith, we unlock the potential to make the impossible possible. This is the key to accessing the supernatural power needed to overcome obstacles and achieve the extraordinary.

Now, let us see how every element of the puzzle that the angel used to answer Mary connects together. In order to walk alongside God, it's essential to have unwavering faith in His Word. Without this belief, no matter how irrational or uncertain His directives may seem, one cannot draw upon the assistance or guidance of the Holy Spirit. And without the Holy Spirit's involvement, one cannot tap into the highest level of power capable of transforming the impossible into reality.

Act 1:8 (AMP)
But you will receive power and ability when the Holy Spirit comes upon you!

Just as in the beginning, the spiritual transmission of creative power between the kingdom of God and the earthly realm was enhanced by the Holy Spirit. When God initiated the creation of heaven and earth, the Holy Spirit of God was present, hovering over the face of the earth, awaiting God's spoken Word of faith to activate the intricate network that facilitated the manifestation of the creative power used by God in bringing the earth into existence.

The Holy Spirit fashioned the network that links the earthly realm to heaven's domain, thus establishing the platform through which we can download the highest voltage of power. This power then enables us to transform the seemingly impossible into reality by downloading heavenly provisions to create whatever we require on earth that doesn't yet exist.

This power includes the power to create wealth, establish peace, enjoy a blissful marriage, successfully raise Godly children in an ungodly environment, command sound health, and everything you can ever imagine. Romans 1:16-19 says "I am not ashamed of the gospel of Christ" (I am not ashamed to associate myself with or be in agreement with anything that

God says). This is what generates the power of God from one level of faith to another.

This is how our faith, the Word of God and the ministry of the Holy Spirit plays a significant role in making impossibility possible. The Word of God says everything is unto us according to the level of our faith and not according to the severity or complexity of our problem.

However as powerful as the Holy Spirit is in this process, the quantity of the power that the Holy Spirit can generate to make impossibilities possible is constrained to the level of our faith. Therefore, for God to make impossibilities possible we have to take sides with Him by believing what He says, then the Holy Ghost will be activated to generate power that makes the impossibility possible.

Act 1:8 (KJV)

But ye shall receive power, after that the Holy Ghost is come upon you: and ye shall be witnesses unto me both in Jerusalem, and in all Judea, and in Samaria, and unto the uttermost part of the earth.

This passage reveals to us that the power that makes impossibility possible is released to you, after the Holy Ghost has come upon you: and you shall become the witnesses that prove that the word works.

We can see the example in the life of Mary. For her to experience the miraculous that made impossibility possible, she had to believe the Word spoken by the angel in order to activate the Holy Ghost which generated the highest level of power that made impossibility possible. Therefore, we too cannot accomplish the impossible or experience the miraculous without the help of the Holy Spirit and without walking by faith.

Why do we need to engage the power of the Holy Spirit? The unction of the Holy Spirit carries the following attributes:

Acts 10:38 (KJV)

How God anointed Jesus of Nazareth with the Holy Ghost and with power: who went about doing good and healing all that were oppressed of the devil; for God was with him.

- The Holy Spirit generates the power that makes impossibility possible.
- The Anointing of the Holy Spirit breaks yokes of impossibilities.
- The Holy Spirit simplifies complex problems
- The Holy Spirit reveals the solution to all our problems. Nobody sees a thing and doubts it at the same time.
- Our faith is activated and doubt disappears when the solution is revealed by the Holy Spirit.
- Moreover, the Holy Spirit is designed to enhance our capacity for revelation.

1 Corinthians 2:10 (KJV)

But God hath revealed them unto us by his Spirit: for the Spirit searcheth all things, yea, the deep things of God.

Romans 8:26 (KJV)

Likewise the Spirit also helpeth our infirmities: for we know not what we should pray for as we ought: but the Spirit itself maketh intercession for us with groanings which cannot be uttered.

Issues don't escalate to the level of problems until we lack spiritual insight. To avoid unnecessary escalation, we have to rely on the guidance of the Holy Spirit, who reveals what we need to know when challenges arise. When we discern the appropriate course of action with the assistance of the Holy Spirit, any challenge loses its classification as a problem.

CONSEQUENCE OF IGNORANCE

Jeremiah 46:17 (NKJV)
They cried there,
'Pharaoh, king of Egypt, is but a noise.
He has passed by the appointed time!'

The children of Israel exceeded their stay in Egypt because they did not recognize that their time to be released had passed and they overstayed and suffered for extra thirty years.

This passage is saying for all those extra thirty years of agony, excruciating pain, intimidation and harassment they had suffered in the hand of Pharaoh, he was just a toothless lion, empty barrel and harmless barking dog. If this truth had been released to them by the Holy Spirit thirty years prior, they could have cried out to God and walked out majestically without fail. Until Israel cried out, they were not released from the bondage of slavery. According to prophecy, the number of days of slavery of the children of Israel was designed to end immediately after they served for four hundred years.

This meant any subsequent raging of Pharaoh after four hundred years is just an empty barrel making empty noise. His power to molest and make them suffer had expired at the four hundred years mark. Unfortunately, the children of Israel suffered for thirty-two extra years because they did not know this.

The toothless and powerless Pharaoh made them suffer unnecessarily because they did not connect with the Holy Spirit on time to show them the schedule of their liberation. This suggests that the Israelites should have departed Egypt and ended their suffering after four hundred years, but their ignorance prolonged their suffering for an additional thirty-two years.

Can you imagine how many Israelites died in Egypt within those thirty-two years and how many children were born as slaves that should not have been so?

In contrast in (Daniel 9:2) Daniel, through the help of the Holy Spirit understood by books that they were not supposed to stay in Babylon beyond seventy years and they were able to get out before seventy years expired. That's what the power of knowledge brings to the table and that's what makes the importance of the power of the Holy Spirit very significant. For thirty-two years, Pharaoh was just an empty barrel that could easily be defeated but the children of Israel did not know. Consequently, some of those things that are intimidating us are also defeatable if only we will subscribe to the ministry of the Holy Spirit to show us the way out.

A life devoid of ignorance perceives problems as opportunities. Indeed, a life liberated from ignorance views problems not as insurmountable obstacles, but as opportunities for growth and advancement. It's important to recognize that a problem is not a permanent fixture or an inherent quality of a situation; rather, it's a temporary state or condition.

In other words, a problem is a fling and not a thing; a problem is just the status of a thing at the time. The revelation provided by the Holy Spirit regarding the solution to impossible problems always makes all the difference. Whenever you know what to do, the status changes from a problem to an opportunity. Whenever you do not know what to do, the status classifies the situation as a problem and escalates it to impossibility when you give up completely.

LEVELS OF COMPLEXITY

Problems have different levels of severity that are dependent on your level of ignorance. The severity of a problem can be listed

listed as low, medium, high, and critical.

The complexity of a problem is not what defines the severity of the problem; The extent of our ignorance dictates the severity level of our problem.

- A low level of ignorance creates low severity of a problem.
- A medium level of ignorance creates medium severity of a problem.
- A high level of ignorance creates a high severity of a problem.
- A critical level of ignorance creates critical severity of a problem.

The revelation driven by the Holy Spirit has the power to rectify all these misconceptions and errors in judgment. Additionally, the Holy Spirit is intended to strengthen and enhance our faith.

Jude 1:20 (KJV)
But ye, beloved, building up yourselves on your most holy faith, praying in the Holy the Ghost

Elizabeth was referred to as someone who had conceived a son in her old age, she was confirmed to be irreversibly barren from all ramifications of life. This was an irreversible case but she overcame all forms of impossibility to conceive a son. In order to boost the faith of Mary, the angel told her to go and hear the testimony of Elizabeth. This way she can validate and embrace the efficacy of the process that produced the miracle. Elizabeth told her, "Blessed is she that believed: for there shall be a performance of those things which were told her from the Lord."

If faith is a non-negotiable requirement to connect with the miraculous for an uncommon breakthrough, then the quality of our breakthrough is according to the level of our faith.

As a direct consequence the quality of our faith is what determines the level of God's performance. Therefore, we need to boost our faith in order to engage God to make impossibility possible. The Holy Ghost is the number one faith booster.

QUICKENING BY THE HOLY SPIRIT

Finally, the Bible says that the Holy Spirit quickens our mortal body. This means that the Holy Spirit translates you from humanity to divinity. This helps us not to operate from flesh whenever we face impossibilities; instead it helps us to operate with our divine nature.

The Holy Spirit has the ability to help us stabilize our emotions in order to help us wait patiently for the manifestation of the Power of God, without losing our minds in the process.

The Holy Spirit strengthens us with power and might in our inner man, this helps us to endure the pain and torture of afflictions so that we don't break down and give up at the edge of our miracle.

Notes

CHAPTER 7

THE POWER OF PERSPECTIVE

One of the reasons God will forever remain all by Himself as the only one in His space as THE MOST HIGH is His perspective and His belief system.

His thoughts and His ways are higher than our thoughts and our ways. No one can ever see things the way He sees things unless you share the same point of view with Him. By "point of view," I mean how He perceives things and the perspective from which He evaluates a matter.

When God looks at things, He doesn't just see things the way they are; He sees things the way they could be because He is seeing things from its beginning to its end all at once. He sees potential in everything and everyone He looks at. One of His attributes is Omnipresent which means He is present everywhere. This statement is tricky because being present everywhere does not just limit Him to every place or space, but also means that He is present in every place, every time, at the same time. In essence He is in the past, the present, and the future.

Isaiah 46:10 (AMP)

He Declares the end and the result from the beginning, And from ancient times the things which have not [yet] been done, Saying, 'My purpose will be established, And I will do all that pleases Me and fulfills My purpose,'

Isaiah 46:10 (AMP)

"Think about this. Wrap your minds around it. This is serious business, rebels. Take it to heart. Remember your history, your long and rich history. I am GOD, the only God you've had or ever will have— incomparable, irreplaceable— From the very beginning telling
you what the ending will be, All along letting you in on what is going to happen, Assuring you, 'I'm in this for the long haul, I'll do exactly what I set out to do.'

This implies that His vision emanates from the beginning of creation to the end at the same time. He can see the beginning and the end of everything and every situation in between at the same time while sitting in one place. Therefore, when He looks at anything or any situation, He not only sees where it started from, or its current state, but He can also see how it is going to end at the same time.
God perceives the entirety of existence from His vantage point of view, discerning the precise placement and purpose of every element. His perspective transcends human comprehension, and His words carry the weight of divine authority, shaping reality according to His sovereign will. Hence, when God declares something to be, that settles the matter, it is established as truth, unfaltering and irrefutable.

To Him, observing all the events of a person's past, present, and future is akin to rewatching a movie that He has already seen before. You already know everything that is going to happen before it plays out. Therefore, if He says you are rich while you are poor and broke, it is because He has seen your future and that is exactly the way it already is. Whenever He says, you are healed while you are still sick or facing death then the reality is that you are healed because that is actually how it is going to be.

If He says your marriage is not going to end in divorce while you are in the divorce court, it will surely end the way He said it would. If He says your child will be great while he is still causing trouble all over town, addicted to drugs or wayward, what God said will take precedence.

If He says you are going to become the next president while you are still in jail, or that you will become a great coach or mentor while you are going through depression and contemplating suicide, whatever He said is what is going to happen. If He says you are going to get married to the most wonderful living being in the world, while you are struggling with all kinds of insecurity and low self-esteem, you had better start getting ready for your wedding. If He says you will have your own child when every reproductive organ in your body is completely dead, and time seems to double over, start buying baby stuff. Whenever He speaks, realize that He is not looking at the things that are seen or the current circumstances, because they are temporal and subject to change, He looks at the things that you are not seeing that only Him can see which are permanent and are the true reality.

REVELATION GIVES THE CORRECT PERSPECTIVE

Every time God speaks He is speaking about a future that already exists; from His standpoint it has already happened.

He is already there in time in the realm of the spirit. It is just a matter of time before we arrive there to witness the physical manifestation. We must be prepared to walk by revelation rather than by mere information in order to fully embrace our journey with God and avoid confusion or losing our way.

God's angle of vision is always the right perspective and it is only through divine revelation that we can see from God's perspective.

Revelation is **Divine Intel** about the future. When we became born again, we were recreated in His image. We were translated from the kingdom of darkness to his marvelous light. That means every attribute in Him including supernatural ability to see from His perspective was reactivated in us and we were empowered to think and function like Him. Therefore, the essence of the new birth is to heal our vision impairments, thus upgrading us by design to operate with the same perspective as Him in the new creation reality.

1 John 4:17 (KJV)
Herein is our love made perfect, that we may have boldness in the day of judgment: because as he is, so we are in this world.

1 John 3:2 (KJV)
Beloved, now are we the sons of God, and it doth not yet appear what we shall be: but we know that, when he shall appear, we shall be like him; for we shall see him as he is.

Therefore, right now, as He is, so are we in this world. Hence, we already have a sound mind that functions with the same perspective like God.

So in order for us to get the same dimension of results like God we need to operate with the same perspective as God.

Godly perspective helps us to think like God and whenever we think like God we are bound to operate or perform at the same level like Him. It is not like God to think shallow impossibility thoughts, God thinks deep possibility thoughts. He **said in...**

Psalm 42:7 (AMP)
Deep calls to deep at the [thundering] sound of Your waterfalls;
All Your breakers and Your waves have rolled over me.

In order to function and get the same order of results as Him we have to function with the same perspective.

That was why He told Peter after he had toiled all night without catching any fish to launch into the deep. Peter's struggle to believe emanates from the faulty mechanism of his perspective. His thought was shallow and could not conceive of possibility in the face of impossibility because he was thinking like an expert fisherman when God wanted him to think like an expert spirit man.

Professionally speaking, expert fishermen don't fish commercially during the day; they fish at night. From experience, if you go out at night and are not able to catch any fish, that means there was no fish in that ocean. If there was no conceivable possibility of catching fish under favorable conditions, then it becomes even more improbable under unfavorable times and conditions. Logically, it was wise to try again the next night but not during the day.

Common sense might suggest that it's pointless for commercial fishermen to fish during the day. However, an uncommon sense, derived from God's perspective, reveals that you can fish at any time when God instructs you to do so. There is an uncommon sense that operates with a Godly perspective level that is deeper than the science of fishery, it can look at an impossible situation and see possibility.

Whatever you cannot see, you cannot conceive and whatever you cannot conceive you cannot deliver.

While Peter was at the crusade by the lake of Gennesaret, he caught a glimpse of revelation from the sermon Jesus just preached. He comprehended what Jesus was implying when he was asked to try again under the most unfavorable conditions, where he had previously failed — a situation deemed practically, scientifically, and technologically impossible. However, based on his current encounter with Jesus and a newfound revelation, Peter went as deep as his recent revelatory encounter took him. He was asked to cast all his nets at once for a catch but he only cast one of his nets which showed how deep he can go and the outcome produced a net-breaking encounter.

Hence, as a believer, you cannot benefit from what God has in stock for you beyond the quality of your perspective as driven by your level of revelation.

God cannot work beyond the level of our perspectives in order not to break our net. This net breaking encounter demonstrates the possibility of what could happen to us physically if God dares to bless us beyond the level of our perspective. The things we care about could break. Imagine if the net represented his mind or his life; something valuable would have been broken at the expense of Peter's life.

PERSPECTIVE

What is perspective and how does it affect our expected result?

- Perspective is your perception of a situation at play.
- My perspective acts as the prism through which I interpret things, defining my possibilities and what they entail.
- Perspective is what leads to the summary or conclusion of your personal interpretation of what you see.

In Summary, your perception is what determines your attitude, or disposition towards the situation in view. These aspects are programmed as your default settings by impulse, without your direct control over them.

Consequently, my perspective of how I see the situation is what determines how I am going to react to the situation. Therefore, my actions and reactions to the situation dictate the outcome I will ultimately achieve. We can confidently assert that your attitude governs your actions, which in turn determine the eventual outcome.

If your actions are influenced by your attitude, and your attitude is shaped by your perspective, then how you perceive a situation ultimately determines whether you react with anger or choose to overlook it.; if I am going to be sad or happy, discouraged or excited. How you see things determines whether you are going to be aggressive or casual and consequently, determine if you are going to win or lose. God forbid that your perspective is faulty, your result will automatically be faulty.

BELIEF SYSTEM

A belief system on the other hand is an ideology or set of principles programmed inside of us that control how we interpret our perception. Your perspective is controlled by your belief system because your perspective will always reference your belief system before coming to its conclusion and making its decision. Your belief system is a repository of programs built to control your decision-making process. They store a series of scenarios and relative approaches or sets of conditions that control how to respond when the scenarios are at play. That means before your perspective jumps to its conclusion, it has to consult your belief system and your belief system will recommend different options of relative actions that could be taken

For example, let's say there's a list of actions deemed disrespectful, and my personal belief system dictates that when someone disrespects me, I should cut them off and maintain a distance from them, perhaps even resorting to holding grudges. However, what constitutes disrespect can vary greatly based on individual personalities, cultural backgrounds, and upbringing.

Consequently, two individuals may observe the same behavior but react in completely different ways. Their response is determined by their unique perspectives and belief systems.

In this scenario, if someone perceives certain actions as disrespectful and opts to hold grudges, they likely consulted their mental list of disrespectful behaviors and compared them against their belief system to decide on a response. If their belief system includes the option to unfriend or hold grudges, then that's likely how they'll react. On the other hand, if another person sees the same actions as insignificant within their cultural context and upbringing, and if their belief system doesn't endorse cutting people off or holding grudges under any circumstances, they would never resort to such measures, regardless of the provocation.

Therefore, if you fix the belief system, you would have fixed the perspective, once the perception is fixed, you will automatically fix the actions that produce the outcome.

As a result, my belief system and my perspective has to be deeper than regular depth to produce an extraordinary result. The bible says that except your righteousness (belief system and perspective) surpasses that of the Pharisees and Sadducees you cannot enter (benefit from the uncommon opportunities that are available in) the kingdom of God.

REPENTANCE & MIND RENEWAL

Indeed, the core message of Jesus Christ centers on the importance of repentance and renewing our minds — a fundamental shift in our thinking patterns — as an indispensable prerequisite to fully experience the benefits of God's kingdom.

Repentance involves turning away from our old ways of thinking and living and committing to a new direction guided by God's principles and values. This transformation of mind is essential for aligning ourselves and values with God's will to unlock the abundant blessings He offers.

By renewing our minds, we undergo a profound internal change that affects every aspect of our lives. We discard negative thought patterns, worldly perspectives, and harmful behaviors, replacing them with Godly wisdom. This renewal enables us to perceive the world through the lens of God's truth and respond to situations in ways that honor Him.

Ultimately, embracing repentance and renewal of our minds is a foundational step towards experiencing the fullness of the abundant life that Jesus promises to all who follow Him. It allows us to fully participate in the blessings, joy, and fulfillment found in living according to God's kingdom principles.

Paul in Romans 12:2 was equally literally begging us not to conform to how others think but to renew our minds with the Word of God. Just like how we renew our license when it expires, we are required to renew our obsolete expired natural thoughts with the current revelation of the Word of God in order to maximize our redemptive benefits.

Jesus talking to the disciples (John 21:6) on a different occasion after different failed attempts to catch fish told the disciples to cast their net on the right side in order to be able to catch fishes where they have failed. That means, my belief system has to point to the right side (God's side / Word's side) in order to catch extraordinary results where others are catching impossibilities.

Therefore, my perspective and my belief system is what controls my response to adversity. How I am going to react per time is based on what side my perspective and my belief system is facing. If they are facing the right side, which is the side of the Word of God, my perspective will be able to see a problem as an opportunity. This way, I will not be offended when I experience it and I will not approach it with a sad attitude. If God delays my miracle, I will not be agitated but understand that it is delayed strategically for my good.

My attitude about time-sensitive issues will be different instead of being anxious, agitated and aggressive because I will know that God is not limited in power to stop negative things from happening. He is powerful enough to reverse them even after it has happened. He is not limited in power to stop anything from dying but is also capable of bringing it back to life from death.

How deep can you think or how deep is your belief system? When I look at the parameters that could naturally define if I am going to be barren or not, what do I see and what conclusions do I draw. When I look at the parameters that naturally define if I am going to be single for the rest of my life or if my marriage will work or not, what do I see and what conclusions do I draw? When assessing the parameters that typically determine whether Iam sick or the severity of the sickness, what do I observe and what conclusions do I draw?

When I look at the parameters that naturally define if I am broke, cannot get out of debt, whether my business will flourish and go global, whether my career will blossom or not, what do I see and what conclusions do I draw? When I look at the parameters that naturally define if I am gonna make it, be successful or not, what do I see and what conclusions do I draw?

When I look at the parameters that naturally define if I am beautiful, gorgeous, cute, old or young, barren or fruitful, what do I see and what conclusions do I draw? When I look at the parameters that naturally define if there is still hope for me or something to look forward to if I should be joyful and enjoy peace on every side, what do I see and what conclusions do I jump to?

A shallow perspective is what makes people jump to the irrational conclusion that their marriage cannot work again. They say things like, I don't love him/her anymore because of how he/she makes me feel; he/she doesn't meet my expectations.

Often, individuals desire their partners to change not for collective or mutual reasons, but for personal satisfaction. This desire for change is driven by selfish motivations rather than a consideration of how the change could contribute to their partner's destiny or purpose.

A limited perspective can lead individuals to hastily conclude that there are no viable solutions to their predicaments, often overlooking potential alternatives or opportunities. The children of Israel faced the red sea while they were being pursued by the host of Pharaoh and thought it was the end of the road for them.

Consider the concept of half full versus half empty, if I say something is half empty then I may become anxious that it run out. But when I say it is half full, I am encouraged that it is on its way to being filled up. Therefore, I can't just bury a case because it is dead! I need to respond to it correctly. There is a chance that I may be able to bring it back to life if I respond to it correctly. It is better to try that chance and fail than not try at all. There will always be a possibility of missed opportunities if I do not try at all.

Revelation access things that are located in the deep while information only gives you access to the shallow ground. That means a life that is based on revelation is a life that shops in the deep and a life that will always get things right. Therefore, with the right perspective by revelation, If I look at failure correctly and respond correctly to failure I can turn it around to an outstanding success; If I look at defeat correctly and respond correctly to defeat I can turn it around to an outstanding victory; If I look at marital crisis correctly and respond correctly to a marital crisis I can turn it around to an outstanding marital bliss. Invariably, in order to turn impossibilities to possibilities, we need to move from a self- centered or world-centered perspective to a God- centered perspective (revelation).

Our belief system is the mentality; an ideology or set of principles programmed inside of us that surrounds what our perspective uses to rationalize what it is looking at and where it is looking to draw its conclusion.

Therefore, if we are looking at a situation with the right lens (revelation) but in the wrong place (wrong belief system), that is, a faulty mentality, our perspective will always get it wrong and so also is our response.

This is exactly what happened to Peter when Jesus asked him to launch to the deep to catch the fish. His belief system could not match up with the level of revelation he received and consequently did not allow him to cast more than one net. The result is that his net broke. In the eyes of man, he caught a lot of fishes but in the eyes of God, he settled for less because his belief system sabotaged him even though his perspective was changed but could not go farther than what his belief system allowed.

Therefore, in order to maximize our divine opportunities which include making impossibilities possible; we need our perspective to always get it right. This means we need a new set of belief systems that goes deeper and beyond all past experiences that are outside the word of God. We need to redirect it to the right side which is the side of the Word of God. We need to get rid of everything and mentality that does not point to the Word of God and supper-impose it with the Word of God.

Notes

CHAPTER 8

FAITH FACTOR ENGAGING THE FORCE OF FAITH

In the previous chapters, I was able to show you that all things are possible and that the things that are impossible with men are possible with God. I went further by saying God can only go or do as far as your eyes can see. In this chapter, I aim to demonstrate the indispensable and indomitable power of faith. It's crucial to understand that God operates within the scope of our faith, as everything responds to faith.

Faith can be described as an aptitude to be convinced beyond reasonable and unreasonable doubt that God will perform what He has promised in His word without fail regardless of the contrast.

Faith centers on your degree of conviction about the efficacy of what God has said about your situation and it finds expression in how you respond to impossibility.

The Bible says that 'The just shall function by faith;' (Romans 1:17) that means that God designed us to function by faith and our default settings must be faith driven. Hence, when we fail to respond to life's circumstances with faith, we undermine the primary purpose and benefits of redemption. It indicates a malfunction in the divine machinery that is meant to produce extraordinary results.

OUR CONVICTION IS PROVED BY OUR ACTIONS

If I am convinced that all things are possible, I don't have to be sad, worry, be anxious, or be depressed whenever my expectations are not met or delayed. If I am convinced that he will work all things for my good, I don't have to be agitated when things have not yet worked as expected. If I am convinced that God has my back and will meet all my needs, I don't have to limit my expectations to what is available or be frustrated by what is not available. I know that, in the end, He will exceed my wildest dreams and provide for me beyond my imagination.

All these and beyond are what faith is designed to fix. Faith is designed to stabilize my state of conviction until I obtain my desired outcome. Nothing is supposed to move me out of alignment with what God has promised when faith is functioning properly as designed.

PLEASING GOD AND ACT OF FAITH

Hebrews 11:6 (KJV)

*But **without faith, it is impossible to please him:** for he that cometh to God must believe that he is and that he is a rewarder of them that diligently seek him.*

This passage says WITHOUT FAITH, IT IS IMPOSSIBLE TO PLEASE GOD! Let us stop here first. The implication is that making choices that pleases God must be our number one priority whenever we face any form of impossibility in order to engage the supernatural. All choices that please God are covenant instructions given as requirements to be met in order to obtain the promises made by God.

Hence, our main task is to react to impossibility in ways that will impress God. Acting in faith impresses God while acting in fear disappoints God. Therefore, pleasing God whenever we face impossibility is our covenant requirement required to attract God's intervention if we want to turn impossibility to possibility. This is the fundamental basis by which faith is established - impressing God by our action.

This means we displease God whenever we don't act in faith, that is why the bible says that anything that is not done in faith is a sin.(Romans 14:23)

For example, If we need God's intervention to be healed of a terminal disease. The only way to engage with God is to be fully convinced that He will heal us, regardless of the severity of the disease. We must refuse to be swayed by the doctor's report but instead stand firm on the promises of God's Word. God is impressed when we believe His report over our doctor's report.

The Bible says, "If a man's way pleases God, He will make his enemy be at peace with him."(Proverbs 16:7) Then if a man's way does not please God, his enemies will continue to be at war with him and prevail against him in all ramifications of life. Based on this understanding, the devil cannot overcome us when we adopt ways that please God, which is the way of faith. However, the devil has the right to continue tormenting us when we subscribe to ways that do not please God, which is the way of fear.

CONSEQUENCE OF ABSENCE OF FAITH

Going back to the statement that says **WITHOUT FAITH, IT IS IMPOSSIBLE!** That means everything remains impossible without faith; it means that all the hassles that we are facing in life that we regard as impossible are as a result of the absence of faith. This means that whatever is impossible is impossible not because it can't be possible but it is impossible because faith is missing in action. Based on this statement, every form of impossibility is a result of the absence of faith. Impossibility can only flex its muscles where faith is absent.

In Mark 9:15-29, we witness the disciples of Jesus grappling all day with casting out demons responsible for a child's sickness, yet failing to do so. When Jesus arrives, he effortlessly casts out the demon. Jesus attributed the failure of the disciples to cast out the demon to a lack of faith and told the father of the boy that "ALL THINGS ARE POSSIBLE IF THEY CAN JUST BELIEVE!" The only thing that can stand between us and making impossibility possible is fear, doubt and unbelief. All things mean ALL THINGS! Including the healing of cancer, paying off debts, healing of emotions, the forgiveness of sin, provision of high-paying jobs, taking your business to global prominence, giving you your own child, making it possible for you to get married to your dream spouse, bringing you out of prison and wiping off your unfavorable history. I could continue indefinitely, providing a list of occasions and evidence demonstrating how God has intervened repeatedly in various circumstances. They are all at the mercy of faith. Faith has no mercy when it comes to dealing with your problems, especially the ones that seem to be impossible. Impossibility is an opportunity for faith to shine. Faith shames impossibility.

On another occasion in

Luke 8:22-25 (NKJV)

22 Now it came to pass on a certain day, that he went into a ship with his disciples: and he said unto them, Let us go over unto the other side of the lake. And they launched forth.

23 But as they sailed he fell asleep: and there came down a storm of wind on the lake; and they were filled with water, and were in jeopardy.

24 And they came to him, and awoke him, saying, Master, master, we perish. Then he arose, and rebuked the wind and the raging of the water: and they ceased, and there was a calm.

25 And he said unto them, Where is your faith? And they being afraid wondered, saying one to another, What manner of man is this! for he commandeth even the winds and water, and they obey him.

The disciples were in jeopardy and were about to perish by the storm and Jesus only spoke to the storm and the storm ceased. The question Jesus asked them is "Where is your faith?" That means the disciples left their faith behind and traveling without their faith. The greatest mistake anyone can make in life is to embark on any journey (marriage, business, career, parenting, academic, e.t.c) without carrying their faith along. Could you imagine what could have happened if Jesus did not bring His faith along with Him to the journey. All of them would have perished of course. The disciple misjudged the basis for the solution and said "what manner of man is Jesus" instead of saying "what manner of faith did Jesus have." The solution was not about the uniqueness of Jesus but was all about the uniqueness of His faith. Faith was present and the storm was disgraced!

1 John 5:4-5 (MSG)

4-5 Every God-born person conquers the world's ways. The ***conquering power that brings the world to its knees is our faith.*** *The person who wins out over the world's ways is simply the one who believes Jesus is the Son of God*

Faith is the antidote for all forms of impossibility. Impossibility is rendered powerless and bows at the mention of faith. Faith is the Power that brings Impossibilities to Its Knees! Praise God!! Impossibilities tremble at the sight of faith!! Therefore, we cannot afford not to bring faith along to any gig or party of "impossibility" events we intend to attend.

Faith is the spank of punishment for any form of impossibility. Impossibilities cannot flex their muscles or misbehave where faith is present.

This scripture is letting us know that adversity only misbehaves when faith is not around just like children only misbehave when the adult is not around. There was a time in my church that I preached this verse of this scripture. I said that faith works just like the way our parents give punishment to troublesome children whenever they misbehave. While I was growing up, whenever we misbehaved, our parents would punish us, which means discipline us. One of such punishments is asking us to kneel down, raise our hands and close our eyes for as long as possible or asking us to pick a pin or to sit like a monkey until it becomes extremely unbearable. Those actions were more difficult to explain, however, just as it sounds, it is a very painful punishment that will set any stubborn child straight. So I told the congregation to exercise their faith any time they face impossibilities by punishing the stubborn problem; asking it to kneel down, raise its hands, and close its eyes. That day a pregnant woman in the congregation that had long passed her due date was in excruciating pain. She caught the revelation and did exactly what I told them to do when she got home. To God be the glory, she gave birth that same day. Thank God for faith in action!

FAITH IS NON-NEGOTIABLE

Going further Hebrews 11:6 says "Without faith, it is impossible to impress God;" anyone that needs the intervention of God must believe. That means that faith is a non-negotiable pathway for anyone that exclusively needs the intervention of God to resolve his issue. No one can impress or gain access to God without faith. Therefore, the force of faith must be engaged for anyone to be able to attract God to his situation.

Faith is not a nice-to-have weapon but a must-have for anyone that needs to have God step into their situation.

Anyone who needs God's help to resolve their issues must believe. Anyone who desires impossibility to become possible must believe that God is who He said He is and will do what He said He can do.

Faith is thus, partnering with God to bring whatever He has said to pass on the earth. Partnering means you do what you are required to do as a proof that you trust that He will do what He has promised that He will do. Faith is also making a continuous effort to line up your ways with the ways of God, that is, adopting the ways or approach of God to accomplish your desired outcome. It's the only way to please him, that is what the partnership is all about; faith in action.

In Luke 18:1-8 Jesus told them a story showing that it was necessary for them to pray consistently and never quit. He said, "There was once a judge in a city who never gave God a thought and cared nothing for people. A widow in that city kept after him: 'My rights are being violated. Protect me!"

Prayer is a platform provided for us to resist or stop all human rights violations and faith is the weapon required to be used to stop it.

Whatever is not right that you don't resist has the right to remain. Like earthly policemen, we are expected to exercise our spiritual constitutional right whenever there is a discrepancy between what we are experiencing, or going through, and what God has promised us.

Faith is the weapon that spiritual rights activists use to get justice or stand up for their rights or what they believe.

Faith is demanding your right to what rightfully belongs to you – The force of Faith stops the violation of both your spiritual and human right.

Luke 18 : 4-9 (MSG)

"He never gave her the time of day. But after this went on and on he said to himself, 'I care nothing what God thinks, even less what people think. But because this widow won't quit badgering me, I'd better do something and see that she gets justice—otherwise, I'm going to end up beaten black and blue by her pounding.'"

6-8 Then the Master said, "Do you hear what that judge, corrupt as he is, is saying? So what makes you think God won't step in and work justice for his chosen people, who continue to cry out for help? Won't he stick up for them? I assure you, he will. He will not drag his feet. But how much of that kind of persistent faith will the Son of Man find on the earth when he returns?"

Luke 18 :7-8 (KJV)

7 And shall not God avenge his own elect, which cry day and night unto him, though he bear long with them?
8 I tell you that he will avenge them speedily. Nevertheless when the Son of man cometh, shall he find faith on the earth?

Luke 18 :7-8 (AMP)

7 And will not [our just] God defend and avenge His elect [His chosen ones] who cry out to Him day and night? Will He delay

[in providing justice] on their behalf?
8 I tell you that He will defend and avenge them quickly.
However, when the Son of Man comes, will He find [this kind of persistent] faith on tho carth?"

Let us define faith further using the passage above; Faith is a pounding force that keeps badgering and badgering God on matters He has promised and never quits until it takes delivery of its desired outcome.

Based on this, faith is a belief system that is resolute about its conviction over what God has promised and will never take no for an answer. In the presence of impossibilities, if you find any promises of God applicable to your situation, faith demands that you remain steadfastly convinced that the Word of God will bring about the outcome you anticipate, or that what God has pledged will indeed be fulfilled, regardless of the time it takes.

Faith is an annoyingly irritating force that pounds its way through any form of impossible barrier in order to obtain what was promised. This means that you use your faith to pound your challenge until it shatters to pieces and moves out of the way for you to obtain the promises of God.

Faith can neither be frustrated nor be stopped by impossibility or any form of barrier or opposition.

Every provision or promise of God is routed through the door of faith.

Salvation cannot be experienced without faith for the Bible says we are saved by grace through faith.

We walk by faith - This means that we are without spiritual legs without faith and that makes us spiritually handicapped and restricted to a wheelchair in the realm of the spirit without faith. Consequently, we can't move in the spirit or go anywhere without faith.

We live by faith - This means that faith is our primary means of living in the kingdom. We are going to be spiritually dead or broke and would have no primary means of income without faith.

Our prayers are answered by faith (Matthew 21:22) "And all things, whatsoever ye shall ask in prayer, believing, ye shall receive." We stand by faith (2 Corinthians 1:24) "Not for that we have dominion over your faith, but are helpers of your joy: for by faith ye stand" Therefore, we are completely stranded without faith just because fulfillment of every promise of God are routed through faith.

WITHDRAWAL OF YOUR DESIRED OUTCOME WITH FAITH

Also, the Bible says in (2 Peter 1:3), God has given you all things that you will ever need to live an extraordinary life in a godly way. But it is deposited in the spiritual bank of heaven and can only be withdrawn by protocols of faith.

What we need to realize is that God has deposited everything we will ever need in line with His promise into the supernatural bank of heaven in the Word of God's account and He expects us to use our faith slip or check to make withdrawals anytime we need to.

That means only those who have the withdrawal slip of faith can make a withdrawal from the WORD bank account where God has deposited everything we would ever need in life.

We're asking for joy, peace, prosperity, salvation, security, sound health, gainful employment, successful business, great family, and emotional stability and He's saying I packaged it in the Word account and I need you to withdraw it with your faith check or slip.

STEPPING OUT OF THE BOAT BY FAITH

Matthew 14:25-33 KJV

25 And in the fourth watch of the night Jesus went unto them, walking on the sea.
26 And when the disciples saw him walking on the sea, they were troubled, saying, It is a spirit; and they cried out for fear.
27 But straightway Jesus spake unto them, saying, Be of good cheer; it is I; be not afraid.
28 And Peter answered him and said, Lord, if it be thou, bid me come unto thee on the water.
9 And he said, Come. And when Peter was come down out of the ship, he walked on the water, to go to Jesus.
30 But when he saw the wind boisterous, he was afraid; and beginning to sink, he cried, saying, Lord, save me.
31 And immediately Jesus stretched forth his hand, and caught him, and said unto him, O thou of little faith, wherefore didst thou doubt?
32 And when they were come into the ship, the wind ceased.
33 Then they that were in the ship came and worshiped him, saying, Of a truth thou art the Son of God.

In the passage above, impossibility was made possible. Jesus walked on the water in the midst of the storm and the wind without sinking. Peter also stepped out of the boat to walk on the same water under the same condition without sinking, while the rest of the eleven stayed inside the boat and missed out because they were afraid of sinking.

Most of us have confined ourselves to a boat that is not going anywhere because we are afraid of stepping out of our comfort zone by faith because of our past experiences.

For example, some of us were abandoned by our biological parents and had to live from foster home to foster home; some were homeless living in the shelter or under the bridge and in the midst of it; some were severely abused, and molested. Some have had to go through tough times, unimaginable sufferings, traumatic experiences, deprivation, segregation, racism, discrimination, and harassment of different shades.

Consequently, we have allowed these experiences to define us, shape our perspectives, control our self-image, lower our self-esteem, influence our expectations about life, and thus limit our chances in life. These past experiences have kept us confined within an invisible boat that lacks the capacity to take us to our desired destination in life, preventing us from exploring supernatural means.

The rest of the disciples, with the exception of Peter, were afraid to step out of the boat by faith. Their fear was rooted in the possibility of sinking if they attempted to walk on water, so they confined themselves within a stagnant boat that leads nowhere and was destined to sink eventually.

However, Peter ignored the threat of the water, the wind, and the storm and decided to use another mode of transportation that was unstoppable and stronger than what the boat could offer. This mode of transportation is FAITH! We walk by faith and not by sight! Faith advanced Peter and Jesus while the boat stagnated its occupants. Praise God the water, the wind, and the storm could neither stop nor drown them.

Walking on water seems to be an impossible option but both Jesus and Peter took their chances and succeeded anyway. This means if the rest of the disciples had stopped using their experience as excuses for their stagnation and got out of the boat that was provided by science, technology, psychology, etc. they too would have equally advanced despite the threat of the opposition.

That is what faith does, faith moves you to take chances on the Word of God, and trust me the word never fails. If it didn't fail Jesus and Peter, it will not fail you too. They were both walking by faith on the Word of God (Using an invisible indestructible boat) in the book of Isaiah 43:2 KJV - When thou passest through the waters, I will be with thee; and through the rivers, they shall not overflow thee: Isaiah 43:2 MSG - When you're in rough waters, you will not go down) over the visible water and they were unsinkable.

They actually used an invincible boat of the Word of God by faith, that was why they were unsinkable! You too can walk on this water! You too are unsinkable if you dare to walk on this water. Nothing will be impossible for you.

PROGRESSIVE FAITH

Faith must be dynamically progressive for life to be exclusively progressive.

The same level of faith that got you into the boat may not be enough to get you out of the boat to walk on water when there is a storm and adverse wind while the same level of faith that got you out of the boat to walk on water may not be enough to get you to your destination if the wind and the storm increases beyond human comprehension.

The same ladder that got you to where you are today may not necessarily be enough to get you to where you are going next. That is why your faith needs to progressively continue to increase in order to get you to where God is taking you to next.

This was the case with the disciples and Peter. Not everyone can go by sea on a boat. A lot of people have a phobia for planes and so also for boats. It actually took a level of faith to trust that a boat will not capside to enter into it. Therefore, the same level that got all of them into the boat was not enough to get them out of the boat even when the boat could no longer get them to their destination because of the storm they encountered on the way. Only Peter was able to exercise another level of faith to come out of the boat and walk on water. The rest preferred to die inside the boat than taking a chance on faith. However, the same level of faith that got Peter out of the boat was not able to sustain him on the water when the intensity of the wind and storm increased beyond what he could cope with. He shifted his focus from Jesus to the wind and storm and his faith failed and he began to drown.

That is why Jesus said to Peter, " O you of little faith." When Jesus attributed the reason why Peter started drowning to little faith, he was not talking about the size of his faith, He was talking about the state or the status of the strength of Peter's faith. Otherwise, He wouldn't have said on a different occasion in the scripture that if you have faith as the size of a mustard seed you can move mountains.

In other words, it implies that you can still do big things with small faith but not with weak faith as long as it is strong enough to make it to the end of its journey.

Weak faith will shipwreck your miracle because it cannot stay long on the field till the end without quitting. This type of faith was deemed weak because it lacked endurance and faltered just before the miracle could manifest. It could not survive the increased intensity of the wind and the storm and thus, could not go far.

Strong faith is needed if you want to go far in life. That's why Abraham had to be strong in faith in order to produce Isaac in old age. Different levels of faith were required for different levels of adversity. The same level of faith that produced Ishmeal was not the same level of faith that produced Isaac. The reproductive organ of Abraham was still functional when Ishmeal was born but that was not the case with the birth of Isaac.

Furthermore, most times, what we think may work against us can be used to our best advantage if we use the power of faith to redirect it. For example the wind and the storm designed by the devil to stop you from going far are allowed by God because it can be redirected to help you go far and faster.

I mean your faith can redirect the wind in such a way that instead of hindering you, it will start aiding you like a wind-aided journey. Just as scientists are using wind vanes to generate power, so also, you can engage your faith to use the wind that is blowing against you to generate power you need to overcome your challenges. Also, just as in athletics, speed can be aided by the wind, your faith can redirect the wind to also aid you and accelerate your journey instead of impeding your journey if your faith is strong enough.

Therefore, you need a higher level and quality of faith that can weather the storms, the winds, and the delays of life in order to successfully take delivery of your expected outcome. Based on this, my faith development needs to increase progressively to match up with the increase in the level of my challenges in order to make it to the end. Since the result will only show up at the end and you need to make it to the end in order to obtain the desired result.

Out of all the things that Jesus could have criticized, he only criticized Peter's faith. He didn't say 'you wicked wind were too weak to hold up Peter', but he said " You of little faith." This means that the weakness of Peter's faith was the major factor that contributed to Peter's sinking.

Most times, we misdiagnose our winds and storms as obstacles and admit that the situation is impossible instead of addressing the weakness of our faith. If Peter's faith had been strong enough, neither the wind nor the water would have been an issue.

The instability of the water and the severity of the wind won't matter if you fix your faith. In most cases, we are frustrated and exhausted because we are exerting our energy in the wrong direction trying to fix the wind and getting no result when God is trying to show us how to fix our faith. Our faith is what is designed to fix the wind.

FAITH IS THE TARGET

Most times, the main issue is not always what you think it is. The misconception of the main issue is just a distraction orchestrated by the devil to prevent you from focusing on the major issue so that he can gain the upper hand in the battlefield. The strength of your faith plays a major role in the battlefield. **That is why the main target of the devil is your faith.** He knows that you will gain an upper hand over him and overcome him once your faith is active. Therefore, the devil will try to exaggerate the problem beyond the divinely suggested solution so he can weaken and paralyze your faith in order to defeat you.

1 John 5:4 (KJV)

For whatsoever is born of God overcometh the world: and this is **the victory** that overcometh the world, **even our faith.**

The trade secret that produces the victory we desire is our faith. So, the devil will do everything within his power to make sure that your faith is completely destroyed to keep you under.

For instance, many of us prefer circumstances to appear favorable before we place our faith in God's ability to make things possible. We require the possibility to seem feasible before we activate our faith. By human disposition, we want cancer or terminal diseases to progressively get better before we can believe that God will get us out of it. We don't want the separation to end in divorce before we can believe God for the restoration of our marriage. As long as the business has not gone bankrupt we can believe God for a turnaround. This is likened to using faith like a credit card.

Just as Peter might have been thinking that if the wind ceased, he would be safe, similarly, if the water could support him, he could advance further in life. We all also have a mindset that thinks we would be able to walk on water successfully and overcome our impossible challenges if only the wind can stop, the storms can cease and the water can become stable.

Unfortunately, this is not how things work in the kingdom. That was why Peter sank despite the fact that Jesus was present at the scene. If the wind and the storm were calm Peter would have continued walking. He was afraid because of the increase in the intensity of the wind and the noise of the storm, and he experienced faith failure. That's how the devil works, he keeps increasing and increasing the pressure and causes the condition of the problem to deteriorate in order to scare our faith to death. We need to be spirit smart and beat him at his game.

Whenever our problem deteriorates instead of improving after we have done everything humanly and spiritually possible, we should realize that what the devil is after is to weaken and break down the strength of our faith. What we need to do at this point is to quickly reposition ourselves where our faith can be reinforced. We need to switch our gear to praising God to frustrate and show the devil that whatever strategy he is using is not working. A time of praise and worship of God creates an opportunity to intimidate the devil; knowing that it is a sign that we are at the edge and we are close to the end.

Jesus successfully walked on water under the same condition without sinking to prove to Peter that the wind or storm was not the problem. The same Peter eventually walked on the same water under the same condition back to the boat without sinking.

Somebody else is walking on what you are blaming for your stagnation. This means that some people are going through the exact situation that you are going through without having to put their life and destiny on hold. The direction and the severity or the intensity of the wind should not have to stagnate your life or be an excuse for why you should stop fighting or stop trying or give you an excuse to give up. Regardless of the direction and the severity of the intensity of the wind you have to be willing to continue to try and be confident that you will win with strong faith.

FAITH IS ALL YOU NEED

Jesus was also using the opportunity to teach Peter how to win without feeling like he needed to have everything in order or have to gain full control over all things that were contrary in order to get his expected outcome. He wanted Peter to realize that it was only his faith that needed to get better in order to guarantee the delivery of his expected outcome, the conditions do not necessarily need to get better.

We all are stranded at the face of impossibility because we are operating on the Thomas kind of faith that wants to see the evidence or positive progressive feasibility before we can believe. But Jesus said that only the people who are able to believe the word of God at face value without waiting for the condition to get better before they can believe are more blessed, that is, they stand a better chance of making impossibility possible.

Your faith has to be alright for your life to be alright!

This suggests to us that the wind and the water would have been of little consequence if Peter had gotten the faith thing right. Everything may not be alright but as long as your faith is alright whatever is not alright will eventually become alright.

He says, "you of little faith", which means your weak faith is the issue. This implies that if you've got this part right this wind would not have been an issue. Therefore, Peter didn't drown in the water because of the depth of the water, he drowned because of the depth of his faith. He doubted because his faith drowned outside its limit. The current level of his faith could not withstand the instability of the water, the pressure of the intensity of the wind, and the storm. That was why Jesus did not need to correct the wind or the water. He only corrected the faith.

BIG BOYS OF FAITH

Therefore, sometimes, when God wants to stretch the limit and strengthen our faith, He allows our situation to go down an unfamiliar path. This is what separates the big boys of God from the small boys of God.

The big boys of God are not just comfortable with eating in the absence of the devil but are also super excited to eat in the presence of the enemy. The enemy that you are afraid of and in a hurry to get rid of are the ones you have not met and defeated before.
You are afraid that he can kill you or create a problem that you may not have solutions for if you don't kill him quickly.

See what David said to King Saul in the scripture below when Saul was trying to underrate his capacity to fight and defeat Goliath;

1 Samuel 17:32-37 (MSG)

32 "Master," said David,"don't give up hope. I'm ready to go and fight this Philistine."
33 Saul answered David, "You can't go and fight this Philistine. You're too young and inexperienced—and he's been at this fighting business since before you were born."
34-37 David said, "I've been a shepherd, tending sheep for my father. Whenever a lion or bear came and took a lamb from the flock, I'd go after it, knock it down, and rescue the lamb. If it turned on me, I'd grab it by the throat, wring its neck, and kill it. Lion or bear, it made no difference—I killed it. And I'll do the same to this Philistine pig who is taunting the troops of God-Alive. God, who delivered me from the teeth of the lion and the claws of the bear, will deliver me from this Philistine." Saul said, "Go. And God help you!"

Therefore, there is a class of people that would not need to worry about the wind, the sun, and the depth of the water. They will walk over them because they command that much respect and have earned authority over them.

They know if they have defeated him before, they can always defeat them any day, any time, anyhow, wherever, and under any condition again and again; what they have been through has equipped their faith with the capacity to produce in and out of season. Read about David's mighty men and their feats of faith in 2 Samuel 23

In summary, the quality of your life is according to the quality of your faith and the quality of your faith is according to the capacity of the strength of your faith. The Bible says that the force that controls the power that makes impossibility possible is our faith.

Faith then becomes the most important factor in the equation of making impossibility possible.

Notes

CHAPTER 9

POWER OF REVELATION

There is a direct relationship between divine revelation of the truth, faith, and our expected outcome. Divine revelation is like divine intel provided by God to show us the best approach to win in the challenges of life. It is like a divine expo required to pass the test we are going to take. (2 Kings 6:8-18). It can also be regarded as the picture of a preferred future or a sneak preview of a coming attraction. Like a teaser from the trailer of a movie that is about to be released.

Nobody doubts what he can see!

The main purpose of revelation is to simplify faith and make it very easy for us to believe. Faith comes when the truth is revealed and faith produces when we believe. He has freely given us all things but we can only have access to them by faith. Hence, everything He has given us remains elusive as long as we live in doubt.

John 8:32 (KJV)
And ye shall know the truth, and the truth shall make you free.

As a result, there is no access to claim what He has freely given us without revelation and faith.
(2 Peter 1:2, Romans 5:2, Ephesians 3:12).

James 1:5-8 (AMP)

5 If any of you lacks wisdom [to guide him through a decision or circumstance], he is to ask of [our benevolent] God, who gives to everyone generously and without rebuke or blame, and it will be given to him.
6 But he must ask [for wisdom] in faith, without doubting [God's willingness to help], for the one who doubts is like a billowing surge of the sea that is blown about and tossed by the wind.
7 For such a person ought not to think or expect that he will receive anything [at all] from the Lord,
8 being a double-minded man, unstable and restless in all his ways [in everything he thinks, feels, or decides].

Doubt serves as a strategic weapon designed by the devil to deflate our trust and belief in God's promises. It undermines our faith, casting shadows of uncertainty over the assurances God has provided. Its insidious influence seeks to ensnare us, keeping us bound so that we are unable to access and enjoy the blessings already bestowed upon us.

No one doubts what is evidently obvious. Revelation serves as a guiding light, dispelling doubt and providing clarity on our circumstances. It reveals hidden truths, liberating us from uncertainty and strengthening our faith. With insight into revelation, doubt fades away, and faith emerges naturally

1 Corinthians 2:12 (KJV)

Now we have received, not the spirit of the world, but the spirit which is of God; that we might know the things that are freely given to us of God.

Revelation's transformative power unveils the invisible, empowering us to believe in and achieve seemingly impossible feats. There are realms and realities hidden from worldly perception that are reserved for God's people to discern. While the world may deem access to what is available in these unseen realms unattainable, God deliberately restricts the access to us through His Spirit. This spirit of discernment bestowed upon us the supernatural ability to perceive the unseen and access realms beyond the physical.

IGNORANCE IS THE ROOT CAUSE

God's people are not suffering because of lack of solution, they are suffering because of lack of knowledge. This suffering continues unabated as long as ignorance persists. Ignorance breeds doubt, perpetuating a cycle of uncertainty that persists without revelation. These shackles of ignorance prolong our imprisonment, confining us to the realm of impossibility.

Everyone's prison is his ignorance. Therefore, there is no extraordinary problem, there is only extraordinary ignorance.

Problems are created in our mind whenever there is doubt and problems mature into impossibilities when doubt is not addressed.

If we take our problems to the supernatural hospital for diagnosis, the divine MRI or Cat Scan or X-ray results will only reveal ignorance as the root cause and divine revelation will be prescribed as a cure for the problem.

Hence, revelation, that is, light, is the most effective recommended medicine for ignorance (John 1:1-5); darkness has no answer for light.

Revelation becomes the cure for doubt. When doubt is cured, faith is activated and impossibilities become possible.

The origin of all problems classified as impossibilities begins when we don't know what to do. Therefore, the things that we tagged as problems are the things we don't know what to do to tackle it. This means the level of our ignorance is what over-rates or exaggerates the complexity of every problem beyond its solution. What you regard as a complex problem that you are sweating profusely to solve is the same thing that someone else would solve easily without sweating.

In the book of John 6:5-6 when Jesus was trying to feed five thousand men aside women and children in the wilderness after three days of crusade; He asked the disciples for their opinion on how to solve this problem. He wasn't asking them because He doesn't know the answer, He asked them because He wanted to assess the level of their knowledge so far. He wanted to test how much they understood the concept of faith since they have been under His tutelage.

Unfortunately, the disciples failed their test miserably. Faced with the task given by Jesus, they considered it entirely impossible. Their perception of impossibility arose from their ignorance of divine capabilities. Restricted by their understanding confined to the natural realm, they evaluated the situation solely through earthly perspectives. They calculated the expenses needed to feed the multitude and concluded, based on their limited analysis, that even pooling together their resources for a year wouldn't suffice to provide for everyone at the crusade.

This is how and why we always miss the divine opportunity! Note that God will never give us a dream we can accomplish by ourselves. We always think that when God gives us a dream that

He depends on us to make it happen, whereas He only expects us to trust Him for supernatural provision that we need while we focus on the natural that we can control.

To the disciples, feeding five thousand people was an impossible mission because they were spiritually blind to divine possibilities and they could not rationalize any possible way to make this happen. They were approaching the problem with information technology using their physical sight and experience instead of divine revelation.

Information technology relies on natural data that focus the possibility of the expected breakthrough on human effort and human discoveries while revelation relies on supernatural data that focus the solution entirely on the promises of God.

They thought they were the ones to make it happen while to Jesus, the task was not a big deal because He knew by revelation what to do and He knew He was not the one that is required to make it happen. So Jesus deferred the problem to the only person that could make it happen and the problem was solved miraculously.

Hence, a challenge is classified as a problem not because it doesn't have a solution; but because we don't know the solution. This is why we always conclude that we have a problem whenever we don't know the solution to the problem at hand. The difference between people who call it a problem and the ones who call it an opportunity is that one knows something the other does not know.

Can you imagine that the solution to this particular problem was as simple as just thanking God and distributing what they have by faith? I would have expected Jesus to call an emergency meeting with God the Father and the Holy Spirit. I would have expected the Trinity to be running around helter-skelter, confused, trying hard to figure out the solution and if they can't find it they throw in the towel but that was not the case.

What they had that was regarded as not enough miraculously became more than enough after Jesus gave thanks and asked them to distribute it by faith. Hence, we can easily deduce that complex problems don't need complex solutions; they only need believers with access to divine revelation and simple faith.

The solution to impossible problems always existed within the realm of divine revelation. However, accessing these solutions required consulting with the divine, tapping into the wisdom and guidance offered by God. This is the way to unlock the insights and revelations necessary to overcome seemingly insurmountable challenges.

WE ALREADY HAVE WHAT WE NEED

Romans 8:32 (KJV)

He that spared not his own Son, but delivered him up for us all, how shall he not with him also freely give us all things?

God has already made available to us and also given us access to what we need. There is nothing we are facing in life, no matter how difficult it seems, whether it is possible or impossible that we do not already have what it takes to solve. We just need to consult God on how to use what we have by faith and it will be multiplied and produce what we don't have if we do need it.

We are complete in Him! Whatever we have currently is all that has been given to us by God and that is probably all we need. We don't really need to worry about what we don't have to achieve our dream, we only need to trust God to use what we already have. Therefore, whatever we don't have should not stop us from obtaining our desired outcome.

2 Peter 1:3 (NKJV)
as His divine power has given to us all things that pertain to life and godliness, through the knowledge of Him who called us by glory and virtue,

If we sequentially analyze the scripture above, we will discover that everything we would ever need to live an extraordinary life in a godly way has been freely given to us.

Thus, as previously discussed, divine revelation is the covenant asset required to access what has already been made available for us; to resolve any issue the devil may bring our way; answer any question, or solve any problem we may have to face in life.

Revelation is the scriptural or spiritual understanding of the Word of God. That is why the Bible says that wisdom is the principal thing, but with everything you have, as if all your life depends on it, **GET UNDERSTANDING!**

Revelation comes when we understand the Word of God, that is, when the mystery of the Word of God is unveiled to us.

Revelation was what Jesus had that made him not panic when the provision was not enough to feed thousands of people. It was what He had when He was cornered by the Sadducees and Pharisees to pay His tax. That also was the foundation of Peter's answer to Jesus' question in Matthew 16:13-19

Matthew 16:13-19 (KJV)
13 When Jesus came into the coasts of Caesarea Philippi, he asked his disciples, saying, Whom do men say that I the Son of man am?
14 And they said some say that thou art John the Baptist: some,

Elias; and others, Jeremias, or one of the prophets.
15 He saith unto them, But whom say ye that I am?
16 And Simon Peter answered and said, Thou art the Christ, the Son of the living God.
17 And Jesus answered and said unto him, Blessed art thou, Simon Barjona: for flesh and blood hath not revealed it unto thee, but my Father which is in heaven.
18 And I say also unto thee, That thou art Peter, and upon this rock, I will build my church; and the gates of hell shall not prevail against it.
19 And I will give unto thee the keys of the kingdom of heaven: and whatsoever thou shalt bind on earth shall be bound in heaven: and whatsoever thou shalt loose on earth shall be loosed in heaven.

The revelation of the Word of God is the key to access the Kingdom's resources. The key that opens every invisible gate to access the promises of God. The primary key that will not allow the gates of hell to prevail against the opportunity that God has offered us in the kingdom.

The revelation of the Word of God is the key required to gain access to the kingdom warehouse where everything that has been made available to us by God is located.

Deuteronomy 29:29 (AMP)

29 "The secret things belong to the Lord our God, but the things which are revealed and disclosed belong to us and to our children forever, so that we may do all of the words of this law.

According to the passage above, what has not been revealed belongs to God and what belongs to God can only be released to us when it is revealed. Hence, until it is revealed, some things are allowed to remain impossible; this is because, without access by revelation, everything that God has made available to us remains under lockdown in the warehouse of the kingdom.

Even though God reserved it for us in His custody with our name written on it, we will never gain access to it without revelation. This is where the journey of faith and revelation meets.

FAITH AND REVELATION: REVELATION STARTS THE IGNITION OF FAITH

As we can see, faith is driven by revelation. Faith that is not driven by revelation is mere positive feelings. It's like a boat by the sea without an anchor. Revelation of God's Word is the catalyst for activating our faith. It represents the supernatural comprehension of God's Word that sparks the ignition of faith's power within us. Our faith is cultivated through continuous exposure to the word of God until its impact is fully comprehended on a personal level. Faith springs forth when the cycle of understanding is fulfilled. This cycle involves not only grasping the Word of God intellectually but also internalizing it to the extent that it becomes the guiding principle of our lives. Then activation of faith now occurs when we achieve this deep understanding of God's Word.

Revelation and faith happen at the same time. Faith erupts when revelation comes. Doubt is destroyed when revelation occurs because you cannot doubt what you have understood. Revelation can be used as the primary source of faith and faith can be used to deliver our expected outcome.

REVELATION IS THE RAW MATERIAL

Based on this, revelation of the Word of God is the raw material for every supernatural manifestation that turns impossibilities into possibilities. Therefore, your primary focus should be on areas where you can invest to get revelation, that is, a supernatural understanding of the knowledge of the truth and radical development of your faith.

This is how it works, as a child of God, we are designed to operate as wordsmiths just like blacksmiths. The same way the blacksmith is skillful with using steel to make so many things of value, by melting and forging them, turning steel, brass, gold, and other species of metals into valuable items, believers, that is, people of faith are also wordsmiths. They are also expected to be skillful in turning the Word of God into items of inestimable value. They are expected to use revelation and faith to turn the Word of God to anything or outcome they desire.

Believers must avoid stereotyping or being dogmatic with the Word of God because through revelation, the same Word can be interpreted in various ways, and each interpretation we believe has the potential to produce different corresponding results.

John 1:1-3 (AMP)

1 In the beginning [before all time] was the Word ([a]Christ), and the Word was with God, and [b]the Word was God Himself.
2 He was [continually existing] in the beginning [co-eternally] with God.
3 All things were made and came into existence through Him, and without Him, not even one thing was made that has come into being.

Here, the Bible says everything that was made was made with the Word of God and later in the chapter it says the Word was made flesh. That means that we can use the Word of God as raw material to make anything we desire in life and we can also turn it into anything we desire when it is revealed and believed.

Everything is as cheap as the quality of our faith.

Therefore, our major focus if we want to maximize our redemptive opportunities, is the progressive development of faith. However, faith is not as cheap or as easy as it sounds. Faith is not an easy weapon to acquire. We don't believe just because we are asked to believe or we wish to believe or decide to believe. We only believe when it is revealed.

This is because it is extremely tough for anyone to believe in the face of impossibility. We can only believe when we have already acquired the power to believe. This means that until we have paid the price that believing costs and we have made the sacrifice required to produce faith, we cannot believe. The easiest way to generate faith is to **pursue divine revelation** by investing in any resource that can position us to keep hearing and hearing in every possible format until the revelation that produces faith comes. If it takes years of education to become who we have become in our career or business today, it will also take some amount of effort to pursue the right spiritual education that is needed to generate the level of faith required to produce our expected outcome.

That is the missing link in the life of current church people. They want to use faith like a credit card or a mortgage system, or a line of credit before it comes. It doesn't work like that in the kingdom. Credit cards are not accepted, only debit cards of faith are accepted in the kingdom. Faith has to come first before you can use it. You need to invest time in His presence to hear and continue hearing before revelation can come to pave the way for the required faith to come.

The things that we regarded as humanly impossible cannot be made possible without knowing what to do and doing it.

Knowing what to do is called revelation, and trusting what we know enough to do it, is called faith.

Therefore, there is no extraordinary problem, there is only extraordinary ignorance and extraordinary doubt.

The extraordinary level of some people's ignorance is what makes things look extraordinarily impossible. Extraordinary ignorance produces extraordinary doubt and exaggerates the problems beyond their solution.

Also, there is no extraordinary solution; there is only extraordinary faith development.

We can use the experience we have gained from confronting and resolving the problem to develop our faith for the next level.

CHAPTER 10

YOUR PROBLEM HAS A PURPOSE

All things work together for good to them that love God and are called according to his PURPOSE.

Another version says "In all things God works for the good of them who love him and are called according to his purpose."

It doesn't say everything will be all good at all times; it says even when it's not all good, God is still working and He won't stop working until it is all good.

The question is, "How do I know He has finished working or how do I know the ending of the story?" The answer is, when it is all good! Therefore, no matter how bad it looks, how complicated it has become, reversible or irreversible, deteriorated or catastrophic, it is not over until it is all good.

The good news is, knowing the character of God, He is the Author and the Finisher and when He begins a project; He doesn't abandon it halfway. He completes it. That means, no case can be closed until it is all good or else you will miss the good part if you close it before the end.

Another way to look at it is that if all things are designed to work together for your good, then everything you have been through, currently going through, or will potentially go through in life, the good, the bad, and the ugly are not wasted. They have a role to play in where God is taking you.

The word **"through"** extracted from the word going-through is literally pointing to the fact that everything that you have experienced in life are pathways and not a destination.

Genesis 50:20 (KJV)
But as for you, ye thought evil against me; but God meant it unto good, to bring to pass, as it is this day, to save much people alive.

Based on the passage above, Joseph acknowledged that the adversities he faced, such as being thrown into a pit, sold as a slave, and imprisoned in Egypt, were orchestrated by the devil to destroy him. However, Joseph recognized that God allowed these experiences to occur in order to bring out the best in him, cultivate valuable qualities within him, and ultimately prepare him for a position of authority in the palace. Additionally, Joseph's trials served a greater purpose, as they enabled him to eventually save others.

Therefore, we can conclude that the evil plans of the devil are what God always uses as raw materials to produce the good things that we desire. This means that all the trash that the enemy dumps in our lives are treasures in disguise; if God allows it, it can be recycled to produce good treasure.

Jeremiah 29:10-11 (MSG)
This is GOD's Word on the subject: "As soon as Babylon's seventy years are up and not a day before, I'll show up and

take care of you as I promised and bring you back home. I know what I'm doing. I have it all planned out—plans to take care of you, not abandon you, plans to give you the future you hope for. Every problem has an expiry date!

This passage summarizes the approach of God on this subject matter. God has an expiry date for every problem. God won't show up until the expiry date, not a day before. This is a good thing to know whenever you are going through a prolonged difficult situation. You need to know that every problem that has a start date also has an end date! However, In the midst of it, God has a plan to take care of you as He promised but He won't intervene even a day before the expiry date. There must be a reason why God allocates an expiry date to all problems and won't intervene before the date. In hindsight and based on previous experience, we can say that the reason centers around the fulfillment of the purpose of the problem. That means that He won't intervene until the problem has fulfilled its purpose. During this season of life, it will appear as if He has abandoned you, it will look like a God-forsaken season, but just when it looks like it's over, God will show up and make all things beautiful. He will never leave you hanging; He will surely come through for you at the right time. Therefore it is expedient for you to learn to patiently wait on Him while the problem is fulfilling its purpose.

GOD OF PRINCIPLE

Why would God delay His Intervention? Does God enjoy watching us suffer? What kind of father will delay His response and intentionally watch His children suffer? This doesn't add up or sound like the compassionate and kind God that we serve.

Proverbs 3:27-29 (MSG)

Never walk away from someone who deserves help; your hand

is God's hand for that person. Don't tell your neighbor "Maybe some other time" or "Try me tomorrow" when the money's right there in your pocket.
Don't figure ways of taking advantage of your neighbor when he's sitting there trusting and unsuspecting.

The passage above is applicable to God too. He won't violate His own principle. God has our best interest in His heart. He will not delay an answer to your problem without a viable reason or without an intention to work it out for our good.

In the passage, God said I know what I am doing! This is a statement that comes out of frustration whenever you are dealing with someone that doubts your ability to fulfill your promise.

God said He's got you! He has it all planned out!! That means that He wants you to chill out and understand that the ugly situation you are going through is part of the plan. He has already envisaged it and He has a contingency plan put in place to salvage it.

When you look at this statement you will realize that the reason why evil is associated with the plan in this passage is that a situation that looks like evil is also included in the package. That means there is always going to be a time when you will go through a situation whereby what He promised you will be completely different from what you are experiencing.

For example, He may promise to promote you and the next thing you see is that you have been laid off from work. This was my situation a few years ago. I was expecting a promotion at work and my boss threw me under the bus on a project. I was disgracefully rolled off the project by the client. I was so sad because I loved the project and it was supposed to be a platform for me to become a manager. This was a disaster! I was expecting a promotion and I was completely removed from the line of promotion because of this incident. Rolling me off a project would not even look good on my performance review at the end of the year and woul affect my bonus.

Just as I was mourning profusely in the parking lot, I received a call from a recruiter telling me about a job opportunity. Ordinarily on a good day, if everything was good at my current job, I would not have entertained the discussion at all. But because I was already disappointed about how I was treated even though I had given my best; I took the call and started working with the recruiter on the job opportunity. To cut the long story short, I was offered the job and was given the position of senior manager which doubled my former salary.

See how God used an evil-like situation to double my expectations. He set me up to trade in the position of a manager for the position of a senior manager and also doubled my salary in the process. That was indeed a better tradeoff and better payoff.

Whenever you are facing a problem, don't be in a hurry to pray it away before it finishes its purpose. Let it complete its job to bring the best out of you.

Furthermore, the problem is designed to push us out of our comfort zone. Some of us may not have left our comfort zone if not for the unbearable pain that was inflicted by our adversity. If God works all things together for good, then, your challenges are oppositions with benefits. Problems, challenges, or oppositions are your friends in disguise with benefits, not your enemy. Therefore, Afflictions, adversities, oppositions, and setbacks, are not your enemies, they are your friends with benefits.

ADVERSITY IS NECESSARY

Faith needs problems, adversities, challenges, and afflictions to develop its spiritual muscles.

Problems and challenges are major equipment that faith uses to develop its muscles in the gym of life.

Faith needs to be strong enough to overcome impossible battles. Therefore, faith needs to register in the gym of life to build its muscles in order to put itself in the best shape to conquer its opponent anytime the call demands a fight.

Romans 4:20-21(AMP)
But he did not doubt or waver in unbelief concerning the promise of God, but he ***grew strong and empowered by faith,*** *giving glory to God, being fully convinced that God had the power to do what He had promised.*

It takes a strong faith to remain fully convinced that God had the power to do what He had promised in the face of impossibility.

We can see the growth in the life of Abraham from the doubt that produced Ismael to the power of faith that produced Isaac. Abraham used his adversity to develop the strength of his faith and was able to overcome the previous doubt, and was rewarded with Isaac.

As a result, Impossibility is also not our enemy. Impossibility is our friend. Impossibility is designed to expand the capacity of the strength of your faith. Hence, anytime we face impossibilities, we need to develop and strengthen our faith instead of backing down.

The scripture says if you faint or fail to live to expectation on the day of your adversity, it is not because the adversity is too strong for you or is impossible to surmount; It is because the strength of your faith is small.

God's performance limit is limited by the limit of the strength of your faith.

In order for your faith to be a high performer and be able to move to the next level, your faith has to increase dynamically and progressively at all times.

God will not bless you beyond what your faith can handle. If all things are possible to those who believe, then everything we can ever get or become is according to the level or limit of our faith. This is not talking about the size of our faith as previously discussed before, it is talking about the strength of our faith.

The level or strength of our faith is what determines the quality of our results.

For every level there is a new devil! That means, in life, as you progress towards higher levels of success, you will always inevitably encounter new levels of challenges posed by the devil eagerly mischievously waiting for your arrival. God, in His wisdom, ensures that you are adequately prepared to confront these new dimensions of spiritual opposition before you reach that stage. Instead of allowing you to face these challenges unprepared, God strategically introduces you to these adversaries beforehand. This approach allows you to become familiar with their tactics and schemes, ensuring that they no longer hold power to intimidate you at any level. By preemptively exposing you to these enemies, God equips you with the strength and resilience needed to overcome them when you ultimately encounter them at higher levels of success. Thus, this best practice ensures that you are fortified and ready to face any spiritual opposition as you advance towards your goals progressively.

Matthew 6:34 (AMP)
"So do not worry about tomorrow; for tomorrow will worry about itself. Each day has enough trouble of its own.

Based on the passage above, the evil works of the devil are limitless and progressive and it never ends.

It means, evil occurrences are inevitable for any believer that has been destined for greatness. The bible says many are the affliction of the righteous. To accomplish its devilish vision, The devil has invented and manufactured evil at different levels enough to spread around daily in progressive order and he is becoming more creative and innovative about it. We just got to learn how to build our faith by converting our adversities to our gym instrument in the weight-building room of life.

The degree of the affliction that your faith can handle is equal to the strength or capacity of your faith.

Therefore, If I want to know how strong my faith will become, I just need to know the size of the adversity I am going through. The caveat to this is that the capacity of our faith is what determines what God can give us. That is one reason why we should never say 'This is too much for me'. Every time we say this challenge is too much for me, we are equally indirectly saying my faith is not strong enough to handle the level of success I desire. Consequently, I am not ready for the next level of blessing. Instead we need to use our afflictions as the weight lifting machine to develop our faith.

This is how it works. There are intentional and discretional spiritual regimens that need to be part of our lifestyle by default in order to keep our faith in required shape. Activities like fasting and prayers, consistent studying of the Word of God, adequate church attendance and intentionally staying in the presence of God. Most of these activities don't come easy naturally for some of us that are not self motivated.

God deliberately guides our desired outcomes through paths filled with seemingly insurmountable challenges. These adversities are designed to instill a sense of desperation within us. This desperation serves as a catalyst, compelling us to engage in activities that foster the growth of our faith. By navigating through these impossible adversities, we are motivated to embrace actions that directly or indirectly contribute to the strengthening of our faith. This intentional process ensures that even those of us lacking self-motivation are prompted to take the necessary steps to nurture and fortify our faith regularly. Through this journey, we safeguard ourselves from missing out on opportunities to enhance the quality of our results, particularly in cases deemed impossible. Thus, by traversing these challenging paths, we not only develop resilience but also deepen our trust in God's ability to orchestrate miracles in the midst of adversity.

Therefore, God uses our desires as an incentive to bait us into making the necessary adjustments that we need to improve the quality of our spirituality and character while at the same time boosting the level of our faith to the required size needed to handle the demands or responsibilities that come with the breakthrough we are seeking.

Without adversity, some of us would not have improved the quality of our prayer life, service, love for Him, the study of the Word, increase our time in the presence of God, and adjust our attitude. Adversity puts us in a desperate mode and desperate people take desperate measures. There are no limits to the level of sacrifices we can make when we are in desperate mode.

PROBLEMS ARE FAITH'S JOB SECURITY

Amos 6:1 (KJV)

Woe to them that are at ease in Zion, and trust in the mountain of Samaria, which are named chief of the nations, to whom the house of Israel came!

This scripture is saying that cursed is anyone that is not going through anything because their faith will have no job to do and if your faith is not working it should not expect a paycheck on payday.

The Bible says whoever will not work let him not eat. Problems provide work for faith to do. That is why the bible says, Faith without works is vain, useless, and unprofitable.

Problems are also our servants, they are employed to work for us and not against us.

Exodus 23:28-30 (AMP)

I will send hornets ahead of you which shall drive out the Hivite, the Canaanite, and the Hittite before you.
29 I will not drive them out before you in a single year so that the land does not become desolate [due to lack of attention] and the [wild] animals of the field do not become too numerous for you.
30 I will drive them out before you little by little until you have increased and are strong enough to take possession of the land.

This passage referred to "problem" as our servant. They serve a purpose, just as the giants, Canaanites, and the Hittites served a purpose in the promised land. They were not left by God to work against the children of Israel but for them. The giants, the Canaanites, and the Hittites are divine vigilantes and security guards. Their job is to make sure that they watch over the land, pay attention and do everything within their capacity to maintain and protect the land against the multiplication of invaders until the children of Israel have increased in number and strength to handle invaders by themselves. They are there to make sure the actual enemy of the children of Israel do not outgrow and overpower them. Their main function is to regulate the ratio of the invaders in proportion to the population of the Israelites. They were employed to make sure that the enemies of the Israelites do not grow in population beyond what they can handle at any given point in time. This statement is very significant. This means that there is a direct relationship between the capacity of the strength of the Israelites and the timing that God had scheduled to drive all their enemies out completely. Whatever number of enemies God may have left behind in our lives are not expected to become our boss. We are supposed to recruit them as employees to fight against potential problems and the responsibilities that come with the solution. **That means you should not be disappointed if all your problems are not resolved all at once, there must be a reason and a purpose. We are expected to use our problems as motivation and inspiration to become better and stronger.**

This is very interesting when you look at how practically this principle applies to us. For example, this means that sometimes God may not take away some sickness until we have mastered how to gain control over our eating habits to prevent obesity which can pose a major threat to our health.

Sometimes God may not restore our job or business to its full capacity until we have gained control over our tendency for extramarital affairs or mastered the habit of making God first in our lives. Sometimes God will not fix all our problems completely until we have made necessary adjustments to our spiritual lives. This is the only way He can guarantee that our success will not become a hindrance to spiritual growth.

Therefore, all problems serve a purpose. You need to understand the purpose of your problem first in order to understand the purpose of your problem first in order to respond to it appropriately. Nothing is impossible with God, however, God will not be rushed to deliver his promises unless He knows we can handle the responsibilities that come with the breakthrough.

I have seen people beg God for promotion at work then they become overwhelmed by the demands of the new job responsibility. People ask for children then they complain; using the child as an excuse why they are not effective in life and in the things of God. Some asked for marriage and now complain bitterly about their lack of freedom.

Embracing your challenges with the right attitude as opportunities is always the best way to maximize the end result. God normally channels the opportunity through this way for your own good; it not only gets you something better, but it also strengthens your faith and helps you to become a better and stronger person.

In July 2007, I was laid off from work for about five months and that was the worst five months of my life. I was going to lose everything. My house, my car, and everything I had labored for was about to go when suddenly He showed up and I got a better job and everything was good again. Little did I know that God had used my experience to groom my faith.

Subsequently, every time I hear rumors of layoffs or an economic downturn thereafter, I was never moved because I had been through it before and I survived.

I always believe that the same God that did it the last time will also do it again. I believed to the point that even if He did not show up and I lost everything, I can always recover them and make the enemy pay back seven times whatever He stole from me.

God used that experience to deliver me completely and I was never intimidated by threats of unemployment again.

PROBLEM SOLVING MAKES YOU A GOD TO PROBLEMS

Instead of hastily praying away your problems prematurely, it's more beneficial to take responsibility and seek solutions through the wisdom of God, regardless of how long it may take. Remember, you are created in the image and likeness of God and have been endowed with the mind of Christ, which is a sound mind. This means you possess the same level of wisdom as God and can reason at His level. As stated in the Scriptures, "Come, let us reason together," indicating that you can rub mind with God and engage in intellectual discourse with God.

Similarly, when Jesus instructed Peter to launch into the deep, it signified the invitation to delve into profound realms of understanding. This implies that you have the capacity to access the depths of divine knowledge. Therefore, there is no problem beyond your ability to comprehend and solve.

Relying solely on others to solve your problems deprives you of the opportunity to learn and grow. Just as a student who constantly relies on a teacher for solutions will never develop independence; seeking external solutions without engaging your own faculties hinders your personal growth and development. Embrace the challenge of problem-solving, knowing that through the wisdom of God within you, you can overcome any obstacle.

The problem you don't solve by yourself always remains a threat to you forever.

A problem left unsolved remains a looming threat to you forever, regardless of whether someone else has resolved it for you in the past. The mere sight of the same problem can trigger panic and anxiety, particularly when assistance is unavailable. However, when you take the initiative to solve the problem independently, you gain invaluable mastery over it.

By navigating the process of problem-solving on your own, you seize ownership of the solution. This empowerment ensures that you are no longer dependent on others to address the issue or any related challenges that may arise. You will be armed with the key to the solution and be equipped to face similar obstacles with confidence and competence.

Having conquered the problem through your own efforts, it loses its power to intimidate or hinder you in the future. You possess the knowledge and skills needed to confront it head-on, ensuring that it never resurfaces as a threat or raises its ugly face against you in your life. With autonomy over the solution, you are liberated from the mercy of others and empowered to navigate challenges with resilience and self-assurance. Therefore, don't be scared of problems; take on impossibility as a challenge!

Proverbs 30:30 (KJV)
A lion which is strongest among beasts, and turneth not away for any;

Philippians 1:28 (AMP)
And in no way be alarmed or intimidated [in anything] by your opponents, for such [constancy and fearlessness on your part] is a [clear] sign [a proof and a seal] for them of [their impending] destruction, but [a clear sign] for you of deliverance and salvation, and that too, from God.

Your problem has a purpose and your problem creates opportunities. Your problem develops your faith! Your faith paves way for His performance. Figuring out the solution by yourself through the wisdom of God makes you the master of the problem.

Notes

CHAPTER 11

ENGAGING THE VIRTUE OF PATIENCE

Hebrews 6:12 AMP
so that you will not be [spiritually] sluggish, but [will instead be] imitators of those who through faith [lean on God with absolute trust and confidence in Him and in His power] and by patient endurance [even when suffering] are [now] inheriting the promises.

The passage above says we should follow the example of those who obtain the promise through faith and patience.

The primary tools we need to take delivery of or obtain the promises of God are **faith and patience.** That means we are being warned that there will be cases where some answers won't come as quickly as we expect. Therefore, if we don't want to miss out we need the capacity to exercise the level of patience required to wait until the delivery date of our expected outcome.

Habakkuk 2:3 (NKJV)
For the vision is yet for an appointed time; But at the end it will

speak, and it will not lie. ***Though it tarries, wait for it;*** *Because it will surely come, It will not tarry.*

Ecclesiastes 3:11 (AMP)
He has made everything beautiful and appropriate in its time. He has also planted eternity [a sense of divine purpose] in the human heart [a mysterious longing which nothing under the sun can satisfy, except God]—yet man cannot find out (comprehend, grasp) what God has done (His overall plan) from the beginning to the end.

God is never late! God's blessings are strategically scheduled for an appointed time. The timing of God is always purpose driven. In most cases, His promises are intentionally delayed for strategic reasons and alignment. If you are blessed and fortunate enough to relentlessly embark on this mission, you will be highly rewarded and well compensated at the end of the mission.

For example, the birth of John was intentionally delayed because it needed to wait for the era of the birth of Jesus Christ. There is no way it could have come earlier.

ndeed, the stories of Joseph, David, and Abraham highlight the principle of waiting patiently for the fulfillment of God's promises. Joseph received his dream at a young age but had to endure thirteen years of trials and tribulations before it came to fruition. Similarly, David waited approximately seventeen years from the time of his anointing to his enthronement as king. Abraham experienced a twenty-five-year wait before the birth of his promised son, Isaac.

In these instances, God's timing was essential for the fulfillment of His plans. Joseph's dream required the unfolding of events, including Pharaoh's dream, to pave the way for its realization. David's period of waiting served as a season of preparation, during which God molded and equipped him for his future role as king. Likewise, Abraham's waiting period tested his faith and dependence on God's faithfulness.

Sometimes, God orchestrates delays to showcase His power and sovereignty. He uses waiting periods to refine our character, strengthen our faith, and align us with His perfect timing. Additionally, God may wait for our obedience to be complete before bringing about His promises, ensuring that we are ready to receive His blessings and fulfill His purposes.

Ultimately, these stories remind us that God's timing is impeccable, and His plans unfold according to His divine wisdom. Though waiting can be challenging, it is often a crucial part of our spiritual journey, leading to greater trust, maturity, and reliance on God's faithfulness.

Can God trust you with a promise designed for a mutual benefit between you and Him that could take many years and would require you to wait?

Based on this fact, patience is not just considered the fruit of the spirit but also a weapon of the spirit that can be used to outlast unforeseen delay.

What are other reasons why God would intentionally delay His intervention?

Let us see the answer in

James 1:2-4 (AMP)
2 Consider it nothing but joy, my brothers and sisters, whenever you fall into various trials.
3 Be assured that the testing of your faith [through experience] produces endurance [leading to spiritual maturity, and inner peace].

4 And let endurance have its perfect result and do a thorough work, so that you may be perfect and completely developed [in your faith], lacking in nothing.

Based on the scripture above, the reason why God sometimes will delay His promise is so that patience can do a thorough work that will enable us to become a total package.

"So that you may be perfect and completely developed [in your faith], lacking in nothing."

That means there is something that God is cooking in your life that He will not remove from the oven until it is done. It's not like a piece of steak that people can afford to eat rare. No one likes to eat uncooked of half-cooked food. You have to be well done before you can be useful to God and others.

The word patience here is endurance or long - suffering; endurance equips you with the capacity to handle whatever life throws at you without breaking under pressure, whereas, faith helps you to be relentless in continuing to do what God requires you to do until you see your happy ending. Most of the instructions may be scary, risky, senseless, or redundant at times but we may not make it to the finish line unless we keep following them till the end and unless we make it to the finish line we cannot receive the trophy.

Have you ever witnessed any quitter in any given race being awarded the winning prize just because he was in the lead at a certain point in the race even though he quit before the end of the race? Likewise, unless we endure to the end we cannot be rewarded.

We also need to know that God is not in the business of fixing situations without fixing you first. Moreover, God usually will first expand our capacity to handle the responsibility that comes with the breakthrough we are praying for before delivering the blessing into our hands so that the blessing of God can make us rich without becoming a burden or add sorrow.

He doesn't want the responsibility associated with the blessing to set you back when it starts showing up. This takes time and He won't fulfill His promises until the fixing job is complete. Spiritual maturity is the indicator of this completion.

My experience with buying my first house in the USA serves as a poignant reminder of the importance of understanding the responsibilities and implications that come with blessings before pursuing them. I initially focused solely on affording the mortgage without considering the additional expenses associated with homeownership.

The realization dawned on me when I encountered a substantial increase in bills, including electricity, cable, trash, sewage, water, homeowners association fees, and lawn maintenance. The unexpected expenses stretched my financial resources thin, forcing me to juggle multiple jobs and rely on credit cards to stay afloat.

The toll on my physical and mental well-being was significant, as working three jobs and maintaining irregular hours left me sleep-deprived and stressed. This experience underscores the crucial distinction between blessings from God and those from the world. Unlike worldly blessings, which may bring unexpected challenges and burdens, God's blessings are accompanied by preparation and empowerment to handle them.

God ensures that His people are equipped to manage the responsibilities and demands that come with His blessings. He expands their faith and strengthens their capacity to receive and steward His blessings effectively.

This preparation prevents blessings from becoming sources of pain, hurt, sorrow or drawback ensuring that they bring joy and satisfaction instead.

Reflecting on my experience, I acknowledge that I should have taken the time to fully comprehend the obligations that come with owning a home and waited until I was financially prepared before proceeding. This lesson highlights the importance of seeking God's guidance and wisdom in every decision, trusting that His timing and provision are perfect.

Isaiah 40:31 (NKJV)
But they that wait upon the Lord shall renew their strength; they shall mount up with wings as eagles; they shall run, and not be weary; and they shall walk, and not faint.

According to the scripture above, the waiting period provides the platform to renew our strength. That means that God uses delay as an opportunity to renew the strength of your faith. You need to renew the strength of your faith to stay relevant supernaturally just like you have to renew your professional license to stay relevant in your career field. Therefore, waiting increases your capacity for endurance. This capacity can be used in different areas of our lives.

The same power generated through endurance is the same power you need to cultivate healthy temperance and self-control. These are the mystery behind the successful deployment of every great attitude.

You have heard that your attitude determines your altitude and that talent can get you to a high altitude but you will need a high-level attitude to sustain it.

This is what the weapon of patience and endurance brings to the table. The same level of strength that you need to use to endure adversity is the same level of strength you will need to exercise self-control against resisting fornication or adultery, lying, cursing, addiction of different types, and abusing your spouse. Therefore, God intentionally delays His promises anytime He wants us to make some adjustments to our character or increase the capacity of our faith.

In some instances, He routes the overflowing blessing that is pressed down, shaken together, and running over through the valley of the shadow of death. Take note, it is only a shadow of death; not death. He uses the simulation of death, (shadow of death) to develop and prepare us for the reserved blessing. Like the shadow of death, problems are not real in the first case, it is just a test. The valley of the shadow of death is a training ground where people are prepared for the type of blessing that makes your cup run over so that you don't mess up and get overwhelmed when you get there.

It is a simulation of the same level of pressure that you are going to face at the next level you are aspiring to get to but in a controlled environment. The purpose of the rod and the staff is for direction and discipline. The staff is for direction while the rod is for discipline and empowerment (remember the rod of Moses).

Understand that the valley of the shadow of death is not a destination, it is a transition to the next level - a table where everything is reserved in overflowing proportion.

The most important advantage of going through this route is not just about what is on the table. It is also about the opportunity that is provided for you to go through the experience that will shape and develop your mentality.

This experience helps you to generate boldness, power, and audacity to eat in the presence of the enemy. Most of us can eat in the absence of our enemy but not all of us can eat in the presence of our enemy. Not all of us can enjoy our blessings while corporate evil is going around us. Examples are the news of the potential impact that recession and inflation could have on the economy and its resultant effects on our jobs and finances, families, policies, and things that affect us directly. While some people can no longer sleep well and enjoy what they are blessed with; some of us are sleeping like babies because we have experienced and conquered similiar before in the valley of the shadow of death.

We went through it patiently without cutting corners. Now, we are confident that if we endured and overcame it once, we can do so again and again. What people regard as stress and pressure is what we see as power and a faith stretcher. The goodness and mercy that others are sweating to pursue will follow you on their own volition. The blessing that you didn't even bargain or pray for will come to you without invitation. This is the ideal position for everyone to be in

Read James 1:2-5 in these following versions of the scriptures, KJV, AMP & MSG. It says don't throw anything away, joyfully count everything! Be excited about every situation that comes your way, the good, the bad, and the ugly.

Everything you will ever experience in life is designed to bring you joy in the end. This means the story will always have a happy ending. All you need to do is develop the capacity to patiently endure it and get your return on investment at the end.

James says, "Count it ALL as Joy!" Therefore, if you restrict your count of opportunities to only the likely or possible opportunities, you have missed the most important ones. Your count has to include both possible and impossible ones in the count.

The most valuable returns always come from the impossible ones. Therefore, make sure you include the good, the bad, and the ugly in the count because all things are designed to work together for your good.

James 1:2-4 (MSG)

Consider it a sheer gift, friends, when tests and challenges come at you from all sides. You know that under pressure, your faith life is forced into the open and shows its true colors. So don't try to get out of anything prematurely. Let it do its work so you become mature and well-developed, not deficient in any way.

Your disposition when tests and challenges come at you from all sides is to get excited instead of complaining and whining and looking for an escape route. We are also advised to be patient not to try to escape prematurely.

Just as the world is filled with diverse cultures and people from various ethnicities and backgrounds with unique characteristics and challenges, so too is our experience with problems; they are diverse and multifaceted. Just as there are Asians, Caucasians, African Americans, and Hispanics, each with unique characteristics and cultures, we encounter a multitude of diverse problems, each presenting its own set of challenges and complexities.

The Scriptures acknowledge this reality, stating that "many are the afflictions of the righteous." This recognition urges us to brace ourselves for a wide array of challenges that may come our way. However, the same passage assures us of God's promise of deliverance from all these afflictions. It serves as a reminder that despite the diversity and severity of our problems, God is faithful to rescue us from every trial and tribulation.

It’s essential to note that this deliverance often requires patience and endurance on our part. We must be willing to persevere through the trials, trusting in God's timing and provision. Through steadfast endurance we fully experience the fulfillment of God's promise of deliverance and emerge victorious over the diverse array of challenges we face.

Most of the scientific breakthroughs benefit from today are the result of people who patiently endured the pain and frustration of countless failures until they had the results currently benefit from. According to the Thomas Edison National Historical Park, "In 1879, he made an incandescent bulb that burned long enough to be practical, long enough to light a home for many hours. When they asked him how many times he failed before he finally succeeded, Thomas A. Edison Quote: "I will not say I failed ten thousand times, I will say that I discovered there are ten thousand ways that can cause failure." If he had not been resilient, we may not have the eclectic bulb today. Exercising patience and being willing to endure until we get results ensures we don't miss opportunities.

Often, opportunities not only yield desired outcomes but also contribute to personal growth and skill development along the way.

Therefore, what the writer of James chapter one is saying is that, when adversity puts your faith on trial and challenges your faith to a fight, do not try to get out of it prematurely. If you approach the fight with the right attitude and don’t quit at the edge of a breakthrough, you will not only have your expected outcome, but you will also become a better and stronger person with the capacity to handle the pressure that comes with the blessing. You become a total package lacking nothing! Delay is not even about you or anything material or physical. It is targeted at breaking your faith so it won't last long enough to deliver your expected outcome.

Jesus said He had prayed for Peter so that his faith doesn't fail under pressure. He didn't pray that Peter would not fail because Peter actually failed his test. This is very significant to this statement. The preservation of Peter's faith was more important to Jesus than the outcome of Peter's test. Jesus knew that Peter could not be considered a failure except his faith had failed. Faith failures are like heart failure. Everything fails when the heart fails so also **everything fails when faith fails.**

According to the Bible, man believes with the heart. Therefore our belief is rooted in the heart, implying that the strength of one's belief is closely tied to the condition of their heart. Hence, when the heart is weak, it struggles to maintain strong faith.

Additionally, scripture warns us that deferred hope — when our expectations are continually delayed can lead to heart sickness. A state of emotional and spiritual ailment. A heart that becomes sickened by deferred hope reveals a fundamental defect that requires repair. Such a heart is unable to endure prolonged delays or setbacks. In essence, a sick heart lacks the resilience needed to withstand delays and challenges, hindering its ability to maintain unwavering belief. Therefore, it becomes evident that true and enduring faith requires a heart that is healthy, steadfast, and unwavering in its trust and hope.

This is why we are required to guard our heart with all diligence so it doesn't become weak as advised in the scripture because it is the factory of matters of life.

The Bible says Abraham was strong in faith. I believe that Abraham had to fix his heart condition after he had messed up to produce Ismeal and become stronger in faith in order to produce Isaac. Just as life ends when the heart fails, faith also fails when our heart fails and the process that produces miracles is terminated when our faith fails. As long as our faith does not fail, even if everything else fails we can still recover.

Hence, it's crucial to recognize that the primary aim of the devil, especially when he employs delays in God's promises, is to target our hearts. His ultimate goal is to discourage us, knowing that our faith is the key to overcoming obstacles and receiving God's blessings.

The devil understands that he cannot thwart our progress unless he undermines our faith. To achieve this, he seeks to weaken our hearts by bombarding us by instilling negative thoughts, discouragement doubts, and fears. The aim is to erode our trust in God's promises and diminish our resolve to persevere.

However, he cannot make a shipwreck of our faith unless he can discredit the Word of God that anchors our desired outcome. We also need to be aware that we don’t just develop patience overnight. We exercise patience because we have a heart that is strong enough to endure to the end.

God can make all impossibilities possible but His promises are scheduled. He makes all things beautiful in His time, we need the virtue of patience to endure until our impossibility is made possible by the power of God.

CHAPTER 12

THE POWER OF MENTORSHIP

Ecclesiastes 1:9 (AMP)
That which has been is that which will be [again], And that which has been done is that which will be done again. So there is nothing new under the sun.

Based on the above verse of scripture, we can deduce that there is absolutely nothing new under the sun.

I Corinthians 10:13 (NLT)
The temptations in your life are no different from what others experience. And God is faithful. He will not allow the temptation to be more than you can stand. When you are tempted, he will show you a way out so that you can endure.

I Corinthians 10:13 (MSG)
No test or temptation that comes your way is beyond the course of what others have had to face. All you need to remember is that God will never let you down; he'll never let you be pushed past your limit; he'll always be there to help you come through it.

There is nothing that we are going through and will ever go through that someone has not been through before.

Isaiah 5:13 (NKJV)
Therefore, my people are gone into captivity, because they have no knowledge: and their honorable men are famished, and their multitude dried up with thirst.

No problem is unique or exclusive; our ignorance makes it so.

Impossibility can accurately be defined as an adverse situation with a yet-to-be-discovered solution!

The reason it is called a problem or impossibility is not that the problem does not have a solution; it is because the solution has not yet been discovered.

Hebrews 6:12 (KJV)
That ye be not slothful, but followers of them who through faith and patience inherit the promises.

If there is nothing new under the sun, trying to reinvent the wheel will be utter foolishness and a waste of precious time. The wise thing to do as suggested by God is to learn from or be discipled by people that are ahead of us who have been through what we are currently going through, or people who have accomplished what we are striving to accomplish.

GUINEA PIGS, SCAPEGOATS OR LADDERS

Some people say experience is the best teacher. I absolutely disagree with this statement. Experience is not a nice teacher. Learning by experience can be costly. It can leave you with scars from avoidable mistakes and failures which proper mentorship could have prevented. It is better to learn from other people's mistakes and failures than to understand them by having to go through them yourself.

Mentorship involves leveraging the experiences of those who have already achieved what you aspire to, using them as guides, examples, or resources to reach your own goals. You don't have to start from where they started, you can start from where they stopped, this way, you can go further than them. This is one of the benefits of mentorship; it helps you to break the current record. Jesus said, "Greater works than what I have done shall you do if you follow my lead."

When Mary was struggling to believe that she could have a baby without having sex with a man, the angel's advice to her was to visit Elizabeth who just went through a similar situation. This serves as a profound example of how God often works through seemingly impossible situations to fulfill His promises. Elizabeth's barrenness; her advanced age and her husband's infertility, presented a seemingly insurmountable obstacle to the conception of a child. Yet, it was precisely within this scope of impossibility that God chose to intervene miraculously.

By directing Mary to Elizabeth, the angel provided her with tangible evidence of God's power to overcome impossible circumstances. Mary witnessed firsthand how God had miraculously enabled Elizabeth, against all odds, to conceive a child in her old age. This served to strengthen Mary's faith and affirm the truth of the angel's message to her.

Hence the angel instructed Mary to go under tutelage to learn from Elizabeth's experience and be mentored by her. This underscores the importance of seeking guidance and wisdom from those who have walked a similar path of faith. Elizabeth's testimony of God's faithfulness and provision served as a source of encouragement and empowerment for Mary as she embarked on her own journey of faith and obedience. Elizabeth taught Mary the principles that make impossibilities possible.

The core advice she was given was that she had to believe

before God can perform. She taught her how to believe whatever God said at face value without questioning or doubting it in order to experience what God has said. She showed her that believing in what God had said is what moves Him to perform it.

So Mary did not have to become dumb or go through every pain that Elizabeth and Zachariah went through to see the fulfillment of what God had promised her. This is mentorship in full display.

Also, Elizabeth and Zachariah still needed to have sex after being healed of impotence and bareness respectively. But in Mary's case, she became pregnant without having sex with a man but solely by believing what God had said. This was a level ahead of her mentor. Moreover, Elizabeth had also been pregnant for six months before she met her; this made her more experienced in going through the challenges that come with carrying a pregnancy to term. Therefore, whenever we face impossibilities, we need to ask God to lead us to the anointed mentor who can help build and nurture our faith to deliver.

Most things we classify as impossible are things that we don't have an answer for. However, there is always someone somewhere who has the answer or is already working on the answer; you can collaborate with them to get the answer easier and faster than you would have gotten it on your own.

It could be as simple as listening to the testimonies or studying the material from people who have encountered breakthroughs in the areas that we are still trusting God for.

Revelation 12:11 (NKJV)
And they overcame him by the blood of the Lamb, and by the ***word of their testimony;***

Luke 22:31-32 (MSG)

"Simon, stay on your toes. Satan has tried his best to separate all of you from me, like chaff from the wheat. Simon, I've prayed for you in particular that you not give in or give out. ***When you have come through the time of testing, turn to your companions and give them a fresh start."***

In summary whatever God has done for someone, it is the least of what He can do for you. All we need to do is to shadow them and use their lessons to navigate our challenges, to help us succeed.

Notes

CHAPTER 13

PRAISE-THROUGH

Master key to open Uncommon doors to the realm of Unlimited Possibilities

Matthew 16:19 (KJV)
And I will give unto thee the keys of the kingdom of heaven: and whatsoever thou shalt bind on earth shall be bound in heaven: and whatsoever thou shalt loose on earth shall be loosed in heaven.

The term praise-through just like it sounds similar to breakthrough is referred to as an aptitude to praise God while you're going through the challenge; in the middle of the battle; inside the fiery furnace of fire; while we are losing, and when what we are experiencing does not match the expected outcome. We are expected to praise God through it on the way to our victory.

Praise-through is the gateway to the realm of limitless possibilities and the master key to unlock all doors. Hence, all open doors are direct products of praise-through.

CLOSED DOORS

Open doors are best explained and understood by understanding what closed doors represent. Closed doors have two sides. One side is where doors are closed, but something can be done to open them, or some adjustments can be made to reopen the door. For example, some doors may have been closed because we messed things up, damaged our reputation, or missed our appointment. Maybe we did not work hard enough, did not have enough, or made bad choices. Whenever such doors close, they can be reopened. Such closed doors are not final because they can be naturally reversed; if we make the necessary adjustments, time may bring back those opportunities.

But when the situation becomes irreversible and no matter what we do physically, such doors are considered to be permanently closed and regarded as an impossibility. They can only be opened with special keys. One of such keys is praise.

On many occasions in the bible, we have seen how just praise, thanksgiving, and worship were used as a divine leveler to level the walls of Jericho that were trying to prevent the children of Israel from advancing on their journey to the promised land. We also see an incident where praise, thanksgiving, and worship were used as a weapon of warfare to destroy and chase away the allied forces of the nations that were militating against the peace, prosperity and the stability of the economy of Israel (2 Chronicles 20). Also, we read in Psalms 67 that praise, thanksgiving, and worship can be used as a divine strategy to expand the doorway through which the earth yields her returns or yields her increase.

Therefore in this passage, we shall see how praise, thanksgiving, and worship can be used as the master key to unlock the doors of limitless possibilities. The door that leads to the warehouse where all things that are impossible on earth but have been made possible in heaven are stored. We serve a God that can open all doors - There is no door that God cannot unlock!

SUPERNATURAL KEY

Every good gift that we ask from God, both possible and impossible, comes from above only (James 1:17). However, accessing the treasures hidden in heavenly realms, those gifts beyond the reach of earthly limitations, requires the use of supernatural keys. These keys serve as spiritual instruments that enable us to unlock the gates guarding the realms where divine blessings and provisions are stored.

Sarah got her child at old age with a non functional reproductive organ. This unstoppable key has transformed countless lives throughout history. It was the very key that unlocked the doors of barrenness to fruitfulness for Hannah, Rachel, and Abraham, granting them the long-awaited gift of children. In their desperate longing, they found themselves barred from the blessings of parenthood, but when this key was applied, the impossible became possible.

Likewise, the city of Samaria faced dire circumstances as famine ravaged its streets, leading to unspeakable horrors. The situation seemed utterly hopeless, with starvation driving people to unthinkable acts of cannibalism. Even the economic adviser to the king could not fathom how a turnaround could be possible within twenty-four hours. Yet, with the revelation of the master key, the unimaginable unfolded before their eyes. The economic adviser saw it without tasting it.

This key, the harbinger of divine intervention, defied logic and surpassed human understanding. It unleashed supernatural transformation, turning desolation into abundance, and despair into hope. Sarah, once barren, now cradling her newborn child, said in amazement, "who would have thought Sarah would give breast milk to her child?" A testament to the miraculous power of the key to unlock closed doors.

Indeed, this key holds the authority to unravel the most formidable obstacles, ushering in a reality where impossibilities yield to divine possibilities. It is the gateway to the extraordinary, the bridge between the mundane and the miraculous. With this key in hand, the impossible becomes not just possible but inevitable, as God's promises are fulfilled beyond all expectation.

OPEN DOORS

Praise God! We serve a God with whom all things are possible, He has the exclusive right to open all closed doors. God has the Keys of David and that gives Him the sole proprietorship to open all doors of impossibility. To maximize the benefits of open doors, you need to understand what it means or stands for, so that you can appreciate it when it happens.

A proper understanding of open doors will change your perspective about impossibilities and revamp your expectation about what God has prepared for those who love and trust him.

An open door is an opportunity made available to grant you undeniable access to your expected outcomes or heart desires that are way out of your reach.

An open door can be a situation where you are friends with someone who offers to hook you up with someone you have crush on who seems way out of your league;

An open door can be an introduction to a high-profile

immigration officer that can positively influence the outcome of your immigration status or application.

An open door can be a reference to the CEO of a Fortune 500 company that you have dreamt to work for and they created a job position to employ you based on that reference. An opportunity to grab what is out of your league was created for you through an uncommon influence.

To unveil the mystery of praise- through as a key to open door, let us review the case study of how the door was open for Paul in an uncommon way in the prison.

Act 16:22-31 (KJV)

22 And the multitude rose up together against them: and the magistrates rent off their clothes, and commanded to beat them.
23 And when they had laid many stripes upon them, they cast them into prison, charging the jailor to keep them safely:
24 Who, having received such a charge, thrust them into the inner prison, and made their feet fast in the stocks.
25 And at midnight Paul and Silas prayed, and sang praises unto God: and the prisoners heard them.
26 And suddenly there was a great earthquake so that the foundations of the prison were shaken: and immediately all the doors were opened, and everyone's bands were loosed.
27 And the keeper of the prison awaking out of his sleep, and seeing the prison doors open, he drew out his sword and would have killed himself, supposing that the prisoners had been fled.
28 But Paul cried with a loud voice, saying, Do thyself no harm: for we are all here.
29Then he called for a light, and sprang in, and came trembling, and fell down before Paul and Silas,
30 And brought them out, and said, Sirs, what must I do to be saved?
31 And they said, Believe on the Lord Jesus Christ, and thou shalt be saved, and thy house.

The center of attraction in this passage is prison and the primary focus of everyone in this prison is for the doors to open so that they can get out and enjoy their freedom. To better understand what the prison represents, we need to evaluate the direct relationship between captivity, closed door, and open door. There is a direct relationship with being in a prison and being in a closed door.

A closed door is driven by a situation whereby you are helpless in every way to grab what you reached out for which is similar to what a prison represents.

Prison incapacitates, arrests, or restricts potentials! It is like being locked in a cage and watching what you strongly desire without being given access to obtain it.

There is a certain level of disability or restriction that is associated with you being incarcerated in the prison that restricts you from gaining access to what you reach out to grab. Most of the things you desire are completely out of reach!

In prison, you don't get what you desire, you only get what is offered!

PRISON EXAMPLES

Low self-esteem - This is a self-inflicted imprisonment. A situation whereby, you underrate or underestimate yourself so much that you feel that you don't deserve some things; believing that they are out of your league, too good for you, or that you don't have what it takes and you count yourself out.

Insecurity - Insecurity is a corrosive force that festers within, breeding envy, jealousy and resentment towards those who appear to be thriving. It erects barriers between you and the success of others, fostering a deep-seated fear of being overshadowed or left behind. Instead of celebrating the achievements of others, you view them with suspicion, questioning how their success impacts your own standing.

This pervasive insecurity leads to a life consumed by suspicion and apprehension, trapping you in a cycle of self-doubt and perpetual fear. You find yourself imprisoned by your own insecurities, unable to embrace the accomplishments of those around you, unable to break free from the shackles of comparison and resentment.

Ultimately, insecurity robs you of the joy of genuine connection and collaboration, as you remain locked in a cycle of competition and mistrust. It is only by confronting and overcoming these feelings of inadequacy that you can begin to truly celebrate the success of others and unlock the full potential of your own journey.

Addiction - these are the things you do privately that you are ashamed of but are unable to stop doing them.

Pride - a state of mind, a sense of superiority where you think you are better than others; reluctant to acknowledge mistakes. Pride inhibits empathy towards others, prioritizing self-interest. Pride blinds individuals to their weaknesses and faults, hindering personal growth and development. Moreover, pride instills a fear of vulnerability, preventing individuals from seeking help and leading to emotional isolation. This strains relationships and stifles opportunities for growth and reconciliation. Pride isolates you from opportunities and meaningful relationships and support networks.

INDICATIONS THAT SHOWS THAT YOU ARE IN PRISON

When a deficiency or restriction in one aspect of your life becomes the reason why another aspect is not as functional as desired. Such as the age limit imposed by society on getting married, age limits, or medical conditions imposed by medicine on having children.

When an aspect of your life becomes a prison, it stifles your potential and constraints your ability to thrive. This can manifest in various forms, such as being married to an insecure spouse who undermines your aspirations out of fear of losing control or dominance. In such a situation, marriage becomes a suffocating environment where your dreams and individuality are suppressed, leaving you feeling trapped and powerless.

Similarly, a career that fails to provide fulfillment, flexibility, or satisfaction can transform into a prison, chaining you to a routine that drains your passion and stifles your growth. Likewise, a business that consumes all your time and energy without offering the freedom to enjoy life or prioritize family can leave you feeling imprisoned by its demands.

Religious beliefs that impose rigid limitations without offering guidance on how to flourish can also become a form of imprisonment, confining you to a narrow path devoid of personal growth and fulfillment. Even the journey of childbearing, which should be a source of joy and fulfillment, can turn into a prison when it hinders your ability to pursue your purpose and live a balanced life.

A situation whereby an unexpected disaster or negative events occurred and left a lasting impact that fundamentally altered your life and restricts your ability to engage in activities you once enjoyed. These events can take various forms, including debilitating illnesses or injuries that abruptly end your career, leaving you grappling with the loss of purpose and identity.

Similarly, the sudden loss of a loved one or job, or a financial setback that drastically limits your options and diminishes your quality of life, making it difficult to pursue your passions or attain the things you desire.

Physical conditions, such as obesity-related health issues, that imposed strict dietary restrictions, prevented you from indulging in foods you love and significantly impacting your overall well-being. In such cases, divine intervention may be necessary to open doors for you to regain the freedom to enjoy life's simple pleasures, like eating without limitations.

Moreover, external factors like financial constraints, lack of education, or societal prejudices based on factors like accent, beauty, spirituality, or immigration status, that impose artificial barriers that inhibit your ability to dream and aspire for more. These limitations can erode your sense of hope and thwart your ambitions, compelling you to settle for less than you deserve.

Traumatic experiences, such as abuse, addiction, betrayal, or profound disappointment, that shattered your self-image and instill deep-seated fears and insecurities, making it challenging to trust others or venture outside your comfort zone. These scars from the past can manifest in negative attitudes, behaviors, or perceptions, further complicating your journey toward healing and self-discovery.

Additionally, past mistakes, such as blemished credit histories or criminal records, can strip away your autonomy and subject you to societal judgments and restrictions that curtail your freedom and hinder your ability to make meaningful choices. Those choice have to be made for you with respecting you input

The most interesting part of serving a prison term is that the majority of people doing time in prison are there for their wrongdoing or bad choices made. However in this instance, few of them were there, not for wrongdoing but for right doing, that is, not for the things they did wrong but for the things they did right. Sometimes doing the right thing can also get you into trouble.

Have you ever gotten into trouble for doing the right thing? You were isolated from influential friends for giving your life to Christ, for not joining them to perpetuate evil; you were dumped by your boyfriend because you refused to engage in premarital sex; a situation that put you in a position where you were tagged as too know, busybody, or spirit coco for being passionate about serving God and doing things by the book. Whenever people tag you like this, the implication is that you would be either isolated or alienated. Whenever you come close, people stop talking, or they simply step aside as if you have been infected with leprosy.

Have you ever served God and instead of the liberty you were promised, it looked like it put you in prison? It controls when you sleep or wake up, invades your space, or disrupts your life completely; controls where you can or cannot go; what you can or cannot drink or offer; what songs you can or cannot listen or dance to; the class of people you can have relationships with as buddies or hang out with as confidants, or inner circle.

Paul said that "All things are lawful [that is, morally legitimate, permissible], but not all things are beneficial or advantageous." Meaning sometimes, some of these choices are not necessarily considered sin. Some things don't have to be a sin to be wrong; it's just that they have the tendency to lead you to sin. That is why the Bible says, "when sinners entice you, do not consent"; "flee from every appearance of evil." Aligning with these precautions make your loved ones alienate you. This can give you a prison impression.

1 Peter 2:20 (AMP)
After all, what kind of credit is there if, when you do wrong and are punished for it, you endure it patiently? But if when you do what is right and patiently bear [undeserved] suffering, this finds favor with God.

1 Peter 2:20 (MSG)
What counts is that you put up with it for God's sake when you're treated badly for no good reason. There's no particular virtue in accepting punishment that you well deserve. But if you're treated badly for good behavior and continue in spite of it to be a good servant, that is what counts with God.

In summary, a prison is a place where you lose the right to your choices. You may have lost all right to your choices in the prison but there is always one choice you cannot lose, that is, how you behave in the prison or how you respond to your imprisonment. This is where getting a divine revelation of the purpose of the situation is very needful.

All things work together for good to them that love Jesus and are called according to His purpose.

Whenever we find ourselves in prison regardless of the root cause, the question to ask is, 'why am I in this prison and what purpose should this prison term serve me'?

If I only see my prison term as isolation from the public or a punishment for my wrong choices, and a loss of privileges, then I am a gallant loser and would have wasted many years of great opportunity.

The positive way of looking at it is that, are there ways that I can make some investment that will add value to my life while I am in prison? Is there something I can do or sacrifices I can make while I am in the prison that would eventually pay off when I get out?

For example, prison can provide an opportunity to have free education and learn new skills. Are you taking advantage of this? How can I allow the prison to transform me positively into a better person so that I will not have any reason to return to prison again? With good revelation that is purpose driven, these are the kind of questions we should be asking ourselves while we are serving the prison terms.

Getting out of prison is not as important as staying out! Staying out is not as important as doing well and maximizing destiny. Also getting out of prison is not as important as getting the prison tendency out of you.

PERSPECTIVE

Back to the concept of perspective! You need the right revelation to get your perspective right! The right perspective will help you get the purpose right. The right revelation will give you the right perspective of the situation so you can respond rightly and maximize your prison terms to the best of your advantage.

Sometimes you are not in prison because God could not stop you from going in, but because He has an assignment for you there. He probably allowed you to go through the prison experience because He wanted to disarm the power of prison threats. He wants the prison to become the least of your threats in life so that the threat of imprisonment could never intimidate you again. Sometimes He allows your worst threat to happen to render its power useless. So the next time the prison hears your name they will tremble and think twice before they target you.

Once the devil knows that what he is doing to you is what will accomplish God's divine purpose, he will never try it again. The best way to get the devil off your back is to maximize any situation He brings your way. If he had known that what he did to Jesus Christ was going to help Him fulfill His purpose, he would not have crucified the King of Glory.

This is what God knows, that the devil does not; what he meant for evil God has planned to turn around for your good. Once the devil discovers that time in prison can get you born again, re-dedicate your life to Christ, earn your degrees tuition-free, isolate you from distraction to write books that will change lives or help destinies, innovate or design the best app and become a better person, he will never mess with your life again.

Once the devil discovers that time in prison would help you improve your prayer life, better your relationship with God, spend more time with God, study the word of God harder, and serve God recklessly, He won't mess with you again!

Therefore the first door that needs to open is the door of revelation that will correct your perspective. We have the mind of Christ! The soundest mind ever! This mind is driven by divine revelation, not situation. Your perspective determines your classification,not your location. The right perspective will help you redefine your classification.

YOUR CLASSIFICATION

This is the case with Paul and Silas when they were in the prison. The bible says that "Paul and Silas praised God and the prisoners heard them!" The passage referred to them by their names without classifying them as prisoners even though they were equally in prison.

They were in prison without behaving like prisoners because

they understood that the prison was not their destination but a bypass. Their location did not define their classification. Their revelation controlled their attitude that declassified them as prisoners.

Where you are or what you have at any stage of your life does not have to define or restrict who you are or what you can become. How you respond to the situation or carry yourself at any point in time is what can determine who you will become.

"I may be sick and not behave like a sick person;"

"I may have no money in my account or even miss my payment and choose not to look broke."

"I may be money broke or body sick but change is imminent as long as my perspective is not sick or broke."

Your perspective controls your inspiration

The right perspective will help you get the right response to the situation!

When you discover the purpose of the problem with the right perspective, you will be able to:

- Switch your gear to joy instead of sadness.
- Be excited instead of being sorry for yourself.
- You will be impressed instead of depressed.
- Organize a praise party instead of a pity party.
- Campaign for victory instead of complaining
- Have a sense of humor or honor instead sense of murmuring
- Be transformed instead of conforming and keeping up with the Joneses.
- Use it to become the best version of yourself instead of

becoming the worst version of yourself.
- You will play the win-win game instead of the blame game.
- You can choose to use it as a tool of change,turning it into a mission field and praise God.
- Instead of praying for freedom from prison, you will praise God for the opportunity to be a blessing in the prison!

Your total freedom is rooted in the purpose! You will praise God for the opportunity to be used to get others out instead of focusing on getting yourself out!

Your prayer changes from being self-centered to being God and people-centered. Remember, God turned around the captivity of Job when he prayed for his friends.

Therefore, having the right perspective is everything; God's perspective is the most right perspective. Divine revelation is God's perspective.

Instead of seeing it as a punishment, you can choose to see it as an opportunity to shine the light of God; showcase the power of God. The disciples were happy that they were counted worthy to suffer for Christ's sake (Act 5:40-42)

The right perspective changed their response, their attitude, and their status. Instead of behaving like the prisoners in prison you will behave like the Governor of the prison. Paul and Silas were in prison without looking like or behaving like the prisoners.

It is like having your body in prison but your spirit is focusing on purpose within and outside the wall of the prison.

You are in prison, not as a prisoner but as someone on a mission!

That means, your body may be in the hospital but your spirit is focusing on purpose.

Your body is in the shelter but your spirit is focusing on the purpose.

Your body is in a chaotic marriage, a foster home, under the dysfunctional parenting of two maniacs but your spirit is focusing on the purpose.

You are jobless or underemployed, single or barren at an older age but your spirit is focusing on what the word of God says about you as related to your purpose.

Your perspective changes your attitude or response. It changes the gear from prayer to **Praise war-ship!** That is how to turn praise into a weapon of Warfare.

POWER OF PRAISE-THROUGH

Acts 16:25-26 (KJV)

25 And at midnight Paul and Silas prayed, and sang praises unto God: and the prisoners heard them.
26 And suddenly there was a great earthquake so that the foundations of the prison were shaken: and immediately

ALL the doors were opened and EVERYONE'S bands were loosed.

Praise may be simple but it is powerful and sophisticated! Praise opens up an uncommon door of opportunities! It opens ALL doors at once, making many opportunities available at your doorstep at the same time. Praise creates undeniable opportunities; praise opens all doors! The following happens when you get in to praise groove:

- It turns what should have destroyed you into what will construct you.
- What should have stopped you to propel you.
- Something that should have disgraced you glorifies you.
- Something that should have denounced or renounced you announces you.
- Something that should have damaged you salvages you.
- Something that should have downgraded you upgrades you.
- Something that should have isolated you, insulated you.
- Something that should have brought you down brings you up.
- Something that should have relegated you elevates you.
- Praise turns looming shame into honor.
- Praise redirects depreciation into appreciation and celebration.
- Praise turns tears to cheers; sadness into joy and satisfaction.
- Praise turns your mourning into dancing, ashes into beauty, pain into gain, not enough becomes more than enough, and disappointments into appoint
- ments.

This kind of praise can break through any barrier or any given door at any time under any circumstances. This kind of praise can break any form of chain, confound and silence any troop of security guard acting as a strongman over your destiny. This kind of praise is called Praise-through.

Praise-through is an upgrade of Breakthrough.

Breakthrough makes things happen with the solicitation of God's help while Praise-through makes things happen without the solicitation of God's help. It gets God to gate-crash your party uninvited!

The Bible says, "God inhabits the praises of his people"; "In His presence is fullness of Joy, and at His right hand there are pleasures forevermore." Praise-through is the type of praise that paralyzes the enemy at the gate of breakthrough.
One of the principles that drives praise-through to produce breakthroughs is the law of "mind your business". This law states that you don't need to worry about the things you can't control. Just control the things you can control and the things you can control will control the things you can't control. Praise-through is one of the things you can control. Praise-through is a game changer
The type of praise that changed all forms of ambient to favorable ambient for the three Hebrew boys, it changed a fiery furnace to an air conditioner.

The woman with the alabaster box changed a foul odor to a sweet-smelling savor. In Goshen, Egypt, it exempted the Israelites from the ten plagues of Egypt and their effect. For Paul and Silas, it set up an atmosphere that God could not resist. It changed the prison to a crusade ground. This type of praise is unconditional praise! There is something about this praise that all of us need to rediscover.

Praise works differently in different circumstances. Anybody can praise God when everything is working as planned but not everybody can praise God when things are not working as planned. Therefore praise moves God differently in different circumstances.

If you want to discover the differences, try praising God amid your problem.

- Praise God when you get i n t o trouble;
- Praise God when it seems you are moving from a frying pan into a fire.

- Praise God in the pit of life.
- Praise God in the prison.
- Praise God when you are broke and have lost your Job.
- When your spouse walks out on the marriage,
- When your child is acting crazy.
- When the doctor's report is pretty bad.
- Praise God on your way to the grave.
- When you lose your house, car, or business, in the lion's den.

Praise-through gets God high! God is a praise addict; God cannot resist your praise! Praise has the same effect on God as weed and cocaine on man. Praise makes God lose control. Praise gets God high in the spirit. Praise moves God to invade your space without invitation or your permission. Praise gets God to show up unannounced.

There are different sides of God with different types of praise; different strokes for different praise.There is a nice side of God and there is a terrible side of God. God shows up with His nice side when you praise him when things are good; God shows up with mercy; grace, and compassion.

But when you praise God in the prison, in the fire, in the storm; God shows up terribly. The Bible says, He is fearful in praise; He is ruthless in praise. Praise moves Him to display His ruthless side. That's what makes God arise involuntarily and the earth quakes unhesitantly; that what makes the foundation of the prison shakes and why His enemy scatters. That is when God enters and the entire earth trembles!

That was the case on this very faithful night when Paul and Silas decided to praise God when no one would have chosen to praise Him. Paul knew the key and used it to his best advantage; God showed up fearfully, and ruthlessly. When the soldiers saw his fearful side, they passed out and went into a coma. They were not sleeping, because if they were sleeping, the earthquake would have woken them up but God showed up fearfully. Fearfully means a full measure of fear; the full dose of His ruthlessness!

A dimension of fear that would cause an earthquake, panic attack, or stroke of the spirit that will not just make your enemy become afraid but also provoke a panic attack, stimulate heat waves, instigate strokes of the spirit and cause your enemy to pass out completely and go into a coma.

When you praise God in the prison, God shows up fearfully! When God shows up fearfully, Poverty, failure, oppression, depression, barriers, bareness, bills, debt, disappointments, witches, wizards, principalities, powers, and spiritual wickedness in high places will pass out.

When God shows up fearfully, chains break, mountains melt and all bands are loosed. That means limitations and restrictions are removed and all impossibilities become possible.

When God shows up fearfully, all doors open on their own volition like automatic sliding doors. Doors of healing, blessing, favor, financial fortune, deliverance, success, progress, acceleration, and divine connections.

When praise goes up, blessings come down. Jesus said, "If I am lifted up in praise, I will draw all men unto me." That means, when you praise him; He will give you a raise!

Praise-through always delivers bigger, faster, and better than what you originally desired. Praise-through opens the one door that opens every other door. Praise-through does not just open the door of perspective but also opens the door of access to

Jesus.

Can you imagine, all doors opened and the bands were loosed and the prisoners were free to go but they refused to go. Why? It was because they got something greater and settled better and that thing is Jesus.

Jesus said in John 10:9 "I am the door: by me, if any man enter in, he shall be saved and shall go in and out, and find pasture."

Romans 8:32 (NKJV)

He that spared not his own Son, but delivered him up for us all, how shall he not with him also freely give us all things?

Romans 8:32 (MSG)

So, what do you think? With God on our side like this, how can we lose? If God didn't hesitate to put everything on the line for us, embracing our condition and exposing himself to the worst by sending his own Son, is there anything else he wouldn't gladly and freely do for us?

He that did not withhold Jesus from us when we needed Him most, how would He not with Jesus freely give us all things! He will not bring us out to ghost us and leave us hanging! With God all things become possible! All the doors were opened and they still refused to go out. Something better must have happened to them that made going out of prison become the least of their priority. That is why going out of prison desperately should never be our only priority but having an everlasting encounter that will redefine our lives.

The fact is that, if they had gone out, they would still have to worry about what was waiting for them out there! They would have to deal with the stigma society would have placed on them; worry about how their criminal record will affect their job credit history,; emotional trauma,; where to live; whether they are going to meet the spouse they left the same way they left them; repair the damage their absence may have done to the children they left behind; friends that will not want to associate with them or marry them. But after the door was opened, there was no need to worry about the aftermath of the prison term! God settled all things automatically. One single door opened all other doors. What a cheap way of having a breakthrough we don't deserve. Praise-through gave them a breakthrough to all doors where all forms of impossibilities can become possible!

I don't know what your condition may look like, it doesn't matter what they may have told you, what kind of report you are holding, your level of disappointment or devastation or betrayal, or the complexity of your situation, but with God, nothing shall be impossible. If only you can believe and apply yourself to all the principles in this book, all your impossibilities will turn to possibilities; for with God, all things are possible!

About The Book

The new birth is an initiation into a world of Limitless Possibilities. You deserve better, there's more, and you can't afford to settle for less when you stand a chance of having it all. All things are possible! Unfortunately, we live in the ocean but seem to die of thirst. We own a food storage facility yet we are dying of hunger. We live in error where servants ride on horses, and princes walk as servants upon the earth.

This book is dedicated to ambitious and determined individuals who are committed to achieving everything that is possible for them to maximize their fullest potential in life. It is tailored for those who possess an insatiable hunger to go beyond the ordinary, to attain more, and to become more than they have ever imagined.

This book is the answer to overcoming all forms of limitations. It will help you to right the wrong, correct all errors in your life, and strategically show you how to beat all forms of limitations, so you can become unstoppable, untouchable, unbeatable, undefeatable, and unmolestible, get the best, and be the best that ever lived on earth.

Welcome to a life of Limitless Possibilities!

Notes

About The Author

Ayodeji Ajayi is currently the Lead Pastor of RCCG Salvation Center in Katy, Texas, USA.

He is a God-fearing servant of God who believes highly in leadership by example and excellence in ministry. He is loving, and kind, and has a strong passion for positioning the unexpected and the unlikely for the prolific move of God to lead them to their ultimate destiny.

He is an IT consultant with an engineering background. He has also worked as a senior manager in a leading corporation in Oil & Gas. He has a degree in Mechanical Engineering and a Master's in Business Administration with Specialty in Technology Management. He is a songwriter, sensational and motivational speaker, and gospel musician. He is happily married to the best woman in the world Layide Ajayi and they are blessed with three wonderful children.

Notes

Made in the USA
Columbia, SC
02 May 2025

57395485R00104